# Bigger Than Me

## *Accounts from the Lives of Victims of Domestic Violence*

*Maureen Crimin Einfeldt*

*Dedicated to all who have encountered
abuse at the hands and voice of one who
professes to love and care for them.
It's not only time to speak out,
it's time for the truths of
your stories to be heard,
believed and validated.*

# *Table of contents:*

# What's the Big Deal?

It's a big deal. *It's a really big deal.*

When someone that has been hurt and harmed *repeatedly* over a long period of time by the mean and destructive words and actions of another, finally feels safe enough and courageous enough to tell what happened to them to someone that they trust, it's a very big deal.

It's *the telling*. It is hard to tell another person the painful, intimate details of unspeakable trauma and hurtfulness experienced from the hands and words of another. Add to this the components of love, trust, and family and you have a story that is so complicated, complex, and confusing that your own words seem unbelievable even to yourself. The fears, self-doubt, and embarrassment of having anyone hear unbelievable truths keep the horrors of these stories hidden, guarded, and protected. Yet, there is help and healing for the teller when these stories are shared, heard, valued and validated—believed, as unbelievable as they are.

It's time to talk candidly and openly regarding this difficult shame-filled, blame-riddled, stigma-consumed, and sorely misunderstood social problem that is rampant in our society. It's time to talk about domestic violence. If we want to understand it and hopefully, eventually eliminate it, we need to identify it and be able to recognize it. Sadly, it is everywhere. *Everywhere.*

We'll talk more about *what it is* in a chapter I have titled, "What it is," just so there is no confusion.

Now, for this learning experience, I am going to focus on one set of this domestic violence issue, the one that involves a man and a woman in the relationship of husband and wife, or a male-female partnership. I realize that there are situations that involve women hurting women, men that are harming men and even where the woman is the primary aggressor in a communal household. I recognize that there are women that are difficult to please and to live with. There are women that create situations of extreme control and tremendous discord through their cruel and abusive behaviors. Women can, in fact, control the men in their lives in the same mean and destructive manner, abusing them emotionally, psychologically, physically and in every other way. Yet, very little is known relative to the statistical facts surrounding the number of men and women that are in a domestic relationship where the woman is identified as the abuser. Fewer incidents of this nature are reported to police for a number of different reasons. For this writing, I choose not to address these. Regardless, due in part to the outstanding statistical studies and newspaper headlines regarding men and women in difficult relationship challenges, I choose to write this book comprised of stories from the lives of women that have been harmed by men.

These stories are true. The stories collected here validate abuse by self-centered men that have used their attitudes relative to *male dominance, male chauvinism,* and what they deem to be *male privilege* to create an atmosphere of fear and control that formulates for women the notion that these men are *Big,* even extraordinarily so. They create this perception insomuch that the victims—those that have been affected by their abuse—perceive themselves to be insignificant and their worth is considerably diminished. This book shares these stories as a voice of validation, exposing the fallacies and misconceptions prescribed to by perpetrators of this violence.

I have chosen to use the identification of those women that have been abused as *victims.* I realize that there are many that are less than agreeable regarding this term and have abandoned it relative to those affected by abuse. They use *survivor* in its place as an identifier that indicates empowerment and reclamation of self. I agree, but not until after victims recognize that they are victims. We'll discuss this a bit later on.

In seeking ways to identify domestic violence, it is helpful to be able to recognize particular patterns in relationships that create a sense of unsafety. I will refer to a tool that has been helpful in identifying patterns of abuse in relationships by professionals and is available to anyone. "The Power Wheel," or what is known as the Duluth Model or the Domestic Violence Wheel of Control, is a great tool to be familiar with. I'd like to add just a little personal note regarding the use of this model. Oftentimes the complete cycle with each chamber and each explanation can be a bit overwhelming as the victim is trying to process the complexity of their abuse. It might be helpful to simplify it through the use of your own drawing of the circle and your own arrows and appropriate notations and identifiers. I have included a simple graphic of the cycle that I am referring to. It can be found in the back of this book. No artistic aptitude or engineering degree is necessary. Circles and arrows. Simple explanations. The ability to use this model with simple words and more personal identifiers written within a simple framework will help individuals in abusive relationships detect patterns and cycles of abuse for themselves and recognize these patterns of abuse in their own relationships.

For more information, here is a website where you can find this: https://www.theduluthmodel.org/wheels/.

I will refer to these cycles, as well as utilizing the help of named individuals as *speakers* in this book. Their stories, in their own telling, have been lightly and gently edited so as to make them more easily and clearly read and comprehended.

If you are seeing familiar patterns and feeling like you might be one that you would call a victim of abuse, there is help for you. What happened or is happening to you or someone you know relative to domestic violence and abuse is no small matter. I would urge you to seek help from your local area women's services or crisis shelter. You can also find round the clock help and support at the National Domestic Violence Hotline. It is a 24/7 confidential source of help and direction. They can be found at http://www.thehotline.org and via phone at 1 (800) 799-7233 and TTY (teletype) at 1 (800) 787-3224. They can help you find local help in your area. Help really is just a phone call away.

As you read this book, you will find a few short chapters before the actual stories begin. Please bear with me. There are some critical "how-to's" and "what-to's" along with some explanations and valuable listening support helps before we jump into the stories. These very important support chapters will help to prepare you for what you are going to experience as one that knows these situations or as one that can help and support someone that is going through situations such as these.

After reading this, you might have a desire to get involved in awareness events, volunteer at your local sheltering services, donate financially or with in-kind services or goods as a way to support and help victims on their paths to becoming a survivor. I so hope you do! For this very purpose, I have taken these stories and I have shortened them and collected them into a script that can be used as an awareness performance tool. Awareness and prevention education is critical in understanding this complex social problem and how we can help those entrapped by it. These stories can be used for fundraisers to generate much-needed funds to help women in difficult situations find safety and even create a better life situation for themselves and their families. *"Bigger Than Me, The Telling,"* is available for this type of awareness. This book as a performance tool is also available on Amazon.com.

On a personal note, thank you for reading this, as the more informed we all are about this difficult societal issue of domestic violence, the better prepared we are to evade, avert, avoid and prevent it when it is possible! And, it is possible.

# Home – *it's where we live*

*Home.* German philosopher, Johann Goethe said, "He is happiest, be he king or peasant, who finds peace in his home."

Who doesn't want a happy, peaceful home? Who wouldn't do all they could to achieve this? So, in this place called home, there should be nothing hurtful, harmful or in any way detrimental to those who abide there. It should be a haven—safe and strong—from anything that would attempt to destroy it. We would never have a thing called domestic violence in a happy, peaceful home. Domestic violence is an absolute oxymoron. Think about it. Domestic has reference to home and family—*all things tender*. Violence is defined as *abusive or unjust exercise of power* causing injury and harm. These two words should never find themselves in the same sentence, let alone as a societal term referring to a widespread social problem.

Home, as we have been told, is where the heart is. We should never feel threatened, unsafe, or in peril in that place where our heart is. Domestic violence should never be. But, there are those who would control, abuse and manipulate others for their own selfish pleasure and personal gain, *even in the home*. As much as we try to find for ourselves and create for our children a home with a feeling that they are loved and cherished, we and they just might meet—along life's journey—one who hasn't been raised this same way for one reason or another. It surely happens! There are those that feign goodness while underneath it all, they are not. Yep. They are out there and they will date and collect themselves with us and those we love—our children—even in our homes. Avoiding them as we may, we might find them. We all do our best.

Home, by all of the best definitions, is a place where there is no place like it. It is that place where we thrive, abide, and reside—in love and safety. We should never be harmed there. It is where we live, not worry about being hurt or even dying. It is where we live.

# What it is

Not only is it difficult to understand this type of violence under the conditions of love and trust, it is also difficult to define. A technical definition of domestic violence might be found as a pattern of assaultive and coercive behaviors that include sexual, physical, emotional, and psychological abuse. Patterns of such abuse can also be seen as financial and economic oppression, creating an unsafe environment for the victim and limiting and prohibiting a domain of any kind. These types of abuse are utilized by authoritative individuals against their intimate partners and children where the perpetrator and victim(s) are currently or have been previously dating, cohabiting, married, or sharing a mutual residence. Simply stated, it is being hurt or harmed in any way by one who is trusted under the conditions of a communal household. Regardless of what it is called and referred to, it is a crime, and those that perpetrate this violence are plain and simply criminals.

For a less technical definition, domestic violence is perpetrated by bullies—hurtful individuals that are consumed with themselves and their own selfish wants and desires at anyone and everyone's expense. These men (remember, we're talking about men here) cannot love another person with a pure and selfless love. He has motives, conditions, and provisions—strings tightly and securely attached. He will control, manipulate, blame, demand, demean, humiliate, dehumanize, devalue, exploit— you name it. If you feel hurt, confused or diminished by it, that's what it is. He will turn, twist and spin your words around in such a way that you don't know what you said and why you said it. You will question yourself and your motives. You will feel as if you have lost your clarity and your own brainpower. You'll feel confused, perplexed, and *stupefied* by your own cognition of any given situation at any given or *un-given* time. That's his plan. These abusers are masterful at creating craziness through turning everything around, blaming you for their choices, using sorrow-riddled, superficially turned-on tears, grandiose-over-the-top compliments, *love-bombing*, insincere flattery, and anything else he can dream up at any given moment to manipulate you. There is no way that you will be able to stay on top of it as it can all change so quickly in his favor. It can go from giving you money to spend, then *flipping his lid* when you spend it. That is just one small example of everyday life with a perpetrator of domestic violence.

I have carefully collected stories with permission and endorsements from the lives of those that have lived this chaos. These stories will illustrate different abuse situations and different illogical circumstances that play out in the lives of victims of this abuse. Though different, these stories are all very much the same in describing how these perpetrators use devious and oppressive means to control the minds and break the hearts of those they say they love. For the victims, it is much like a scenario where you *think* you know the rules of the game, but just when you think you do, the rules change. The game spinner for turns or the "color-changing wild card" only work for him—when he says so. Then the rules change again, and again, and again.

If I have painted a picture of confusion and distorted perception, I have done well. Domestic violence and abuse—the *why's* and *what do you do's*—is mind-boggling at best. None of any of it makes sense to normal, logical thinking people, and it is that much harder to see clearly amid the distractions and confusion they create. One thing we do know: it is wrong. It is difficult—even next to impossible (okay, it's impossible) to navigate alone. Remember that hotline? Yeah, call it. They can clear up a lot of the confusion when you seek and engage in the help and assistance these professionals provide.

# The Names Have Been Changed

I have named each story with a name. And again, for clarity, I have also chosen to refer to those affected by this abuse as *victims*. I would love to be able to use the term, *survivors* in this, as this term and personal identifier denotes strength, fortitude, and determination relative to those that find their way out of these violent life circumstances. Survivors of abuse are all of these things and so much more. But not all those that find themselves in these violent situations survive or even *thrive* after living under these conditions. For this writing, I will refer to those caught up in these violently abusive life tangles as victims—*victims with names*.

The *survivor-identity* comes after the victim sees another's actions as detrimental to their personal safety. And, not all that find themselves in the midst of all that comes with abuse are identifiable as *survivors*. Allow me to be clear. There is no shame in being a victim. It is powerful to claim to be a victim in the sense that it is the first step in the realization that someone else's actions have impacted and compromised the victim's safety. You—the one impacted by the abuse—are first a victim, *then*, after reckoning with the effects of the abuse, reclaiming yourself and mentally transitioning to self-safety—become a survivor. Claiming the identity of being a victim of another's harmful actions is a powerful way of disclaiming your part in what happened when so often those abused put so much, *even all*, of the blame on themselves. Victim first, *then* survivor. There is no offense intended by my use of these difficult and often interchangeable identities.

As we know, victims of abuse are not nameless, faceless and void of definitive and immeasurable value. They have names, they have personalities, individual talents and virtues. They are as unique as there are names that name them. The names in these stories and other descriptive identifiers such as numbered children, home situations and work/family characteristics have been changed to protect their uniqueness and *plain and simply*—their names.

Now, as a way of protecting those that have shared their very poignant and extremely personal stories, these stories have been written in such a way as to guard and protect the innocent, rendering their stories to be *fictitious,* as stories go. Some of these stories have also been written, adjusting the extreme and incredibly difficult realities of graphic words and horrifically unbelievable— yet so very true—descriptions of unspeakable abuse so as not to offend or deter readership. Yet, these omitted words and these unrecounted actions are no doubt the actual audible and very visual situations that occur for victims of this abuse.

Some may read these stories, seeing themselves. You very well may see a little of yourself or someone you know and care about. You may see an abuser you know as so many of these situations are typical and classic in domestic violence relationships. If the story reads like yours, by all means, put your name in that place! Give them *yours,* if it helps. If you see yourself or someone you love in this, realize that this could be you, them, or someone you care about. These victims and scenarios are real situations as these things happen to women daily, hourly and even by the minute all over the place. They are real—*uncomfortably real.*

Nonetheless, these stories have been adjusted so as to protect the real stories and real people that have shared them.

It is a difficult thing to feel vulnerable and share hard things even if these things will help someone else, but these *tellers* want to help others. If, by chance, you see something in a story that feels familiar whether you are a sister, brother, parent, child, friend, clergy or acquaintance of someone that is being abused, that Domestic Violence Hotline is for you, as well. Without help from individuals that truly care and truly love those in these difficult situations, victims would lose hope for life to get any better.

# The Invaluable Value of Validation: *The Telling*

Have you ever had a secret situation that you couldn't tell—one that you couldn't tell anyone? *Aaahhh! The agony*! The weight of carrying such a burden! It is so hard! And then, the immense feeling of relief when you find that the "secret ban" has been lifted! It's safe to tell! You can tell, and it's all okay! Someone else knows and the responsibility of carrying it is over! You are no longer alone! *You are free and it is safe to tell!* Holding onto secrets can be so stressful!

Seriously. Secrets can be extremely stressful for the *holder-of-the-secrets*. Holding secrets is a survival skill necessary for most victims of domestic violence. They live their lives daily feeling the fear and anxiety that accompanies holding and keeping relationship-determining, safety-securing, and even life-threatening secrets. Victims of domestic violence hold the secrets of their own abuse while also protecting the secret deeds of their abuser. Domestic violence is a two-sided secret that is the worst kind of double-edged sword. The secrets that victims hold can cut either way—any way—at any time. Victims hold secrets that wreak emotional misery and torment on their mental, emotional, and physical health. Carrying such secrets can break hearts and weaken spirits. They truly do. Holding such secrets is excruciating in every way, but somehow victims do it. For them, silence is sometimes easier, if you can imagine that. It is easier to hold the secrets of abuse than it is to tell someone about them. It's *the telling. The telling* has consequences.

Victims of domestic violence know about consequences. What they know is that they really *don't know.* They live with the fear of unpredictable outcomes regularly. They know all about *walking on eggshells* and avoiding anything that might *upset the applecart.* They know all about *treading on thin ice, walking on broken glass* and *balancing on a tightrope.* Holding secrets is a means of getting through the daily torture of living with an abuser. Victims live in fear that anything they do or say could put them in serious danger. The abuser builds an imaginary *concrete-razor-wired-wall* around the secrets of their abuse. *The telling* has a price. Oftentimes, the price is exorbitant—so very high —and the cost requires payment over an undetermined time frame with collateral that can even threaten their safety or the safety of those they love.

If perchance, the secret of the abuse was to find its way out of the confines of the concrete wall, someone has to *pay.* The price required in *paying* can come in many different forms, ranging from physical to verbal and emotional battery and everything above, beyond, and in between. It has no bounds, no predictable time constraints and there are no conventional speculation guides to tell what *the price* might require. Keeping all of this in some semblance of a very delicate balance, the victim becomes the guardian of the secrets at the peril of their life and the safety of their children. While playing the role of the guardian, the victim becomes the prisoner at the same time. The secret keeps them captive. They don't know who they are anymore as the person that they are diminishes to become what they have to be in order to survive. It is all very complicated, but, though it is complicated, it becomes a way of living for those under the control of a domestic violence perpetrator. For the abuser, it's a head gamer's utopia. For the victim, it is a game with no rules and no possibility of ever winning. It is living while slowly dying inside.

Now, imagine with me that you have a secret—one such as this. This secret, if you tell it, could hurt you on one hand or hurt someone you love on the other. Remember, *the telling* has sharp and significant consequences that you have no control over. There are so many *what-ifs* and *what-thens*. There are so many things to wonder and worry about. What if you tell what you know and then the person you confide in doesn't believe you? What if you tell someone and then they think badly of you? What if they turn against you? What if you scare them off because what you tell is too hard for them to deal with? What if the telling of this thing makes them feel some responsibility to you that they don't want or need? What if they tell someone else and then who knows what might be told and who might hear about it? Who would listen and understand? Who could you trust with such a precarious secret?

Let's say that the secret involves possible life and death safety concerns: situations that could go either way. Someone might have to go to jail or someone might have to testify. Worse yet, someone might die. *The telling* involves revealing truth about someone who has more power than you do. They, because of the *power* they hold, are *bigger than you*. Even though what you know might in some ways give you power, you are powerless because of the consequences related to telling. *The telling* has stark consequences. So, you choose very carefully who you might feel safe enough to tell. You realize that if you tell, and the person you tell about—the person with power—finds out that you told, you could be in serious trouble. If you tell, and the person that you have told doesn't believe you, you may lose their trust and even your credibility, and your reputation might be damaged in the eyes of that person.

Who can you tell with the greatest likelihood of believability and the least tendency to tell someone else? You need someone who will listen and believe *the secret*, no matter how *unbelievable* it might seem. And, having listened to what you have told them, they can't get too upset or overly concerned so as to cause any contention or distress. They must be safe enough that they understand the risks that you have taken in *the telling*. They must understand how difficult this is and how very fragile you are in offering this information to them. They need to be safe physically, emotionally, and even more safe for you in their ability to maturely listen to all you need to share. It would also be an added benefit for you if they would be able to provide a place of safety and protection for you in case your whole world starts to crumble and crash all around you. This is an exceptional person you are seeking because there are so many risks involved.

*The telling* has such complicated consequences. Yet, *the telling* is the key reason for *not telling*. When you look at *telling* with this perspective, it is easier to see why these secrets remain secrets. It is easier to suffer the consequences of silence than to suffer the consequences of *the telling*. Oftentimes, these victims can't even talk—literally. They can't talk. They have been *shut up* and told that they are stupid and anything they say is ridiculous, so they stop talking. Who would believe them, as dumb as they are? *Who would ever believe them!*

So, what would make *the telling* less *costly* and yet more *valuable* in terms of cost for the victim? What would make telling the secret beneficial, even a valued asset that the victim can tally rather than a *cost*? I would assert that it is when the victim feels *valued* that the price on their own self-esteem increases. We've heard that there is strength in numbers. For victims of abuse, the strength in numbers is being more than themselves alone. Value comes in feeling *accompanied*. The value comes in the form of a safe and trusted ally. It comes in the value and power of being believed.

There is nothing worse than feeling alone. It's hard, dark, and frightening. The deepest feelings of despair and hopelessness envelope any sense of safety you may have when you are alone. Having someone to forge through the darkness with us takes away the seclusion, isolation, and fear of loneliness. Having an ally, a friend—*a listener*—dissipates the loneliness. *If only there was someone that you could tell!* You need someone who would simply listen and believe. And who doesn't need that? *The telling,* in the safe and secure environment of an ally, brings indescribable relief to the one holding the secret. The amazing physical and emotional relief of telling someone who listens and genuinely cares cannot be expressed. Everyone wants to be believed. Believing is especially valuable in creating a sense of safety for victims of domestic violence. The more safe they feel, the more they talk.; the more they talk, the more help and support they are able to garner. And the more they talk, the more they hear themselves tell things that they, themselves, need so very much to hear. They need to *tell*. But why tell if no one is going to believe you? They need to be *believed*. They need to be validated.

If you are in the position of being the trusted friend that an abuse victim needs to tell their secrets to, it is important to realize how very difficult it is to tell these things. You have been selected for this very trusted confidence. You are a key component for safety, but there is a certain way to listen that confirms to the *teller* that you are listening. Some call it *reflective listening*, but for this purpose, I will call it what it is: *validation*. Validation, as a listening tool, involves the ability to really hear and understand what the other person is saying through their words and their body language. It is the ability to *get it*. While listening, you reflect back to the person that is telling you things by looking at them, nodding in an affirmative manner, and expressing to them that you do, indeed, understand. Through your own words, your tone-of-voice, your body posture, and your verbal affirmations, the victim knows that they are understood. In an effort to clearly validate to your friend that you are an active, connective listener, it is important to paraphrase and summarize for them what you understand.

Three important and very key components of being a trusted listener are found in these three elements that we'll discuss a little more later on:
1) **Listen.** Listen without judgment.
2) **Believe.** Believe what she is saying is the truth.

3) **Support.** Support her in her decision whether she chooses to leave or she chooses to stay.

Women, different than their male counterparts, need and seek validation. This is why women value girlfriends. Women talk to other women. That is how they share thoughts, opinions, and feelings. Girlfriends validate what *normal* is. Conversations that might come up involve such things as three-year-olds and pacifiers, nursing age margins, what age is best to talk about girl-boy things to your pre-teen, along with a myriad of other normal marriage and family dilemmas. Women wonder about when and if to say something to their guy about the *piddle on the back of the toilet*, the smelly gym bag, or what a real date consists of when her husband checked the date off the list when he accompanied her to the grocery store! Women seek normalcy, and one very safe way to do this is to find out what their girlfriend's experience is and weigh their experience against that. As one who is selected as a friend, or *validator* in the case of a girlfriend's violent home life, it is important to validate normal as definitely not what she is living. This is very difficult to do, as validating is a crucial listening and reflecting skill. Listen carefully to all that is said before offering opinions and directives. Validate carefully those things that are normal, such as the fact that her husband might be tired after a long workday. That is normal. Hitting you because he is tired *is not*.

As an ally, it is critical that you are prepared to do these things. Realizing these things, here is a little caution. When you hear a horrific story of a terrible occurrence, it is so very easy to get caught up in the calamity of the event. You, the ally, need to remain calm. It is also easy to be angry at the abuser and refer to him by some very unsavory names. It is important that you resist the temptation to do this. I'm not saying that he doesn't deserve this, but there might be a better time for this than at this moment. Right now, you, the ally, cannot get caught up in *him*. It is about *her* right now, and that is your focus. Calmly take any focus and any of your effort off of him, and spend your energy validating her.

He'll have his time later. Validate her and her worries, concerns, fears, and her basic need to be listened to through your attention and focus *on her*. This is critical. This is where the importance of *validation* comes in.

Here is an example of what I mean. I have chosen Laura and Karen to help me illustrate this. Laura will serve as *the one abused* and Karen will serve as the *ally*.

> **Laura**: "I am thinking about leaving Allen."
>
> **Karen**: "You are thinking of leaving?" (reflecting)
>
> **Laura**: "Yes. He hit me and pushed me into the wall last night, hitting my head really hard. I collapsed and felt light-headed for a moment."
>
> **Karen**: (taking a breath to calmly respond) "I am so sorry, Laura. Are you okay?" (With compassion -- this could be pretty bad, by the way. You want her to feel safe to tell more.)
>
> **Laura**: "I am now, but I'm scared, and I am worried about what else he might do."
>
> **Karen**: "I am glad you are okay. How can I help you to feel safe? What would you like me to do that would help you feel safe?" (validating her through a sincere desire to help)

Validation allows Laura to talk about what she needs. She needs to feel that what she says is important enough for you, the ally, to listen to her. As Karen validates Laura's words and feelings, it helps her feel as if Karen *gets* her and understands her; it also helps her feel supported. Laura needs to know that what she is conveying makes sense to Karen. It will also help Laura feel more calm and feel settled enough to relate more of what she needs to say. And Karen doesn't immediately go after Allen. Laura now. Allen later.

Again, for clarity, validation of the victim's secret allows them to feel a sense of freedom *from* the secret. *Belief is relief*! You don't need to provide answers or solutions. Just listen. The more safe and validated victims feel in the eyes of their trusted ally, the more safe they will feel to tell. And the more safe they feel to tell, the more they will talk. The more they talk, the more they will hear themselves and not only hear themselves, but understand and make sense of the craziness that living with secrets has created for them. They are strengthened by their own voice and they become stronger as they listen to themselves tell their story. Hearing themselves tell what has happened to them helps them realize how wrong the abuse is. The more they talk, the more powerful they become. They aren't feeling as *small* and insignificant anymore. They are more empowered to make choices when they don't feel judged or criticized. The more empowered, the more clarity they will garner for themselves and their frightening situation.

As an ally, your support is critical in securing a feeling of safety in your friend as she leans on you for support. You can be instrumental in her ability to step away from the abuse and find strength in herself. You need to realize and remember that even though you may see clearly what she should do and how she should proceed, this is not your decision. Respect her choice, no matter what it is. It is so important that you listen to her and her concerns and worries so that you can find out what she needs. Realize and be prepared for the fact that she may choose to go back after telling you that she is done, finished, and through with all the hurt and abuse. It is still her choice and you need to be satisfied and self-assured that you did all that you could. Don't get mad or upset or express any ill feelings that might serve to burn that bridge that you have built on that trusted foundation with her. She may need you again, *the next time.* Even if you do not agree with her, respect her decisions. *Simply listening* is the first frame in the validation framework. Your listening can validate the need for safety as any form of domestic violence is wrong. All of this said, quite frankly, you can't put a value on validation. *It is plain and simply invaluable.*

# "Tiptoe" — Dancing the Dance of the Secondary Victim

Consider this story:

"I am the sister of a victim of an abusive man. I am what is classified as a *Secondary Victim* of Domestic Violence. My sister has been emotionally tormented and physically harmed repeatedly by her abusive husband. It is crushing me. I have contacted a crisis counselor at the women's shelter where she lives. That is how I learned of my own victim status. I have been trying to help my sister find the courage to get out of this relationship while at the same time secure in her the knowledge that I love her. This is so hard! I can't just say what I think like I used to. I have to be so careful that I don't say the wrong thing and ruin what I once had, which is a safe relationship with my sister. I don't like him at all, but I can't say anything. Several of our family members have expressed their concern for her safety and their obvious ill feelings toward him. They love her and it hurts them to see her being hurt. She leaves him and then she goes back. It hurts them when they try so hard to do what she wants, then she changes her mind and goes back to him. When they've told her how they've felt, she acts hurt and pulls away from them. She can't see that they want to help her; she only hears how they feel about him. She becomes pretty defensive. We all love her, but it's so hard not to express our worries and fears for her. My parents are losing patience with her as they have sacrificed their time and resources to help her only to have her return to him so many times. It is so hard for me to try to represent her in a positive light to all of them when she chooses to stay with him. It is all her choice. I am so afraid for her and for her children. I am afraid for me, too. I am afraid of getting too close or too involved, yet I am afraid that if I do nothing, I won't be there to help when she really does need me. Since she has pushed everyone else away, I have realized that I, too am in a difficult place that could end abruptly. I want her to see me as safe for her and for her to trust me. I am also terrified that if her husband knows that I am trying to help her get out, he will cut me out of the picture altogether. It is so difficult to stand by and watch while feeling so helpless."

Pretty hard to read and hard even to imagine, isn't it? It's heart-wrenching to be in that *secondary* spot. Clearly, there are very few things harder than seeing someone you care about trapped in an abusive relationship and feel like you can't do anything. You watch and wonder how to help, what to say and where to begin. You go back and forth. Should I say something? Should I keep quiet? Should I help? Should I mind my own business? Should I be bold or should I be careful? You carefully *tip-toe* around conversations, saying what you safely can without offending or pushing your loved one away. Do I step in? Do I step out? Do I speak up? Do I stay silent? It is *excruciating* to know that the abuse is continuing, not knowing what to do and how to help. You are scared for them; terrified that if you don't say something, they might get hurt, yet knowing that your friendship or sisterhood could be in jeopardy if you say what you feel they need to know. You don't want to pry, push, or cause your friend or family member to distrust you or see you as a threat to their happiness. It is scary but even as frightening as it is, you may even want to somehow rescue them, get them out, and help them to safety, but this aggressive action might also backfire with consequences that oftentimes end up on police records. No one wants that. So, you tiptoe very carefully. Simply by virtue of the love and friendship you have with the abused, you become what is known as a *secondary victim of domestic violence*.

You, the secondary victim, are in a very delicate position. As blatantly obvious as it may be to you, your friend may not even realize that she is being abused. You may need to carefully identify this for her by saying, "I'm concerned about you." You may also need to identify for her the reasons for your concern. You care about her happiness and she doesn't seem to be happy. If she seems to be responsive and non-defensive, you may be able to lead her to help and resources for victims of abuse. Then again, as these things sometimes go, she may resist your help. Don't persist or become aggravated, simply leave that door open by being there. She may come to a point where she is ready to talk or ask for your assistance, and since you opened the door, she might, with your help and support, take a step in. Helping a victim get out of a bad relationship feels very much like you are doing a *tip-toe dance* on a thin, tight wire. You have to step carefully, knowing that if you step too forcefully, you could create a serious imbalance in your relationship. Note here the concept we have just gone over in the chapter on validation relative to "reflective listening." As you listen, rephrase her words to her so that she knows that you understand, then continue to listen.

Here is a little more insight regarding the 3 ideas in *listening* to consider when you find yourself *dancing the dance* of the secondary victim of hopefully helping them to leave a violent or potentially violent relationship:

1) Listen. Listen reflectively, reflecting what she is saying back to her. As I shared before, as you listen, rephrase her words to her and continue listening.

The victim may very well still have feelings of love and attachment to the abuser and hope for a positive change for the better in the relationship. This is normal, but to you, it may seem totally illogical. Realize this. She might, very well, still love him. Even if she does leave, she may go back several times. National statistics indicate that domestic violence victims average 7-8 attempts at leaving before finally making a move to get out for good. Leaving takes time, patience, and love for the helper and real *guts and courage for the abused*. It takes time.

For victims, oftentimes staying seems so much easier because it is what they know how to do. There are so many unknown consequences with regard to leaving. The unknown is frightening. Leaving is very frightening. Carefully ask her what her fears are. Don't ask *why* she is frightened, but *what* her fears are. These fears might include housing displacement, financial dependency, the safety of her children, and her fear that he will become more angry with her. These are very real fears for her and she needs you to validate how real they are. Reflect back to her what she said, expressing your agreement that this is very frightening. By doing this, she now has a *buddy*—remember? *An ally!* She is not alone in her fear. This is important! You, too, are frightened at the prospect of these things—*BUT*—you *can* help her. Let her know of your support and the support of others through even the most difficult times. *And* your concern for her supersedes your feelings about him. Again, *don't even mention him*. Your concern is for her, her children and getting them safely out of this difficult, frightening situation. Help her to see your concern for her's and their safety and your love for her (and the love and concern of others that love her) as an important reason to leave.

2) Listen as if her life depends on it *because it does*. Your ability to listen—really listen—will be key to your friend's ability to hear herself. She may carefully and guardedly tell you things that you absolutely have to have your very best *poker face* on while hearing it. You cannot be emotionally bowled over or surprised by it. Listen and then emotionlessly *reflect*. Reflecting her words after you have heard them completely will allow her to sort things out for herself. Carefully, unemotionally, reflect back to her, "So, what you are saying is that he checks the bank balance every hour, and he also checks the odometer on the car each night when he gets home?" She may affirm this with a quiet "yes" or a nod. This is a good time for the best word in any language. Here it is: "Hmmmm." A nice "hmmmm" at the end allows your friend to hear her own words *swirl around* her own realm of understanding. This will allow her to make sense of logic and illogic regarding her relationship. She needs to process what she has

told you and hear its echo in her own ears. Again, to re-emphasize, hearing herself can help save her from stepping back in when she is faced with the situation she has now shared with you. She will be better at seeing it as abuse by her own definition. This ability to define things for herself could save her life.

*By the way, it's a great word, "hmmmm." You can give it as many *m's* as you'd like. It can be applied to so many things depending on the influx you give it. Hmmmm. It's a great word.

Now, consider this third idea:

3) This is not your battle. It is hers. Your investment in her leaving can't be more than hers. If you step in too much, anything that goes wrong becomes all of *your* doing. You just might get the blame! You are no longer helping when she sees you as *intruding.* You need to protect yourself by staying healthily a few steps far and away from the center. You are an outsider until the victim steps out on her own clearly to where you are. Even then, respect her choices. Remember, this is not about you. You can and will have feelings, opinions, and perspectives on this, but it is not yours. This is her battle. She chooses. Don't take what she chooses personally. Support her, realizing that she may come back to you on another such occasion and need your wisdom when she chooses to employ it for herself.

Alright. Once she chooses to leave, Law Enforcement and your local Legal Services help are critical in helping to keep your abused friend safe. There is help and your local women's shelter or crisis center can give you direction as to what is available in your area.

Remember: This process takes time, and it can be hard to watch the repeated episodes of leaving, then going back. As a secondary victim, you may feel frustration, fear, and impatience. It is not uncommon for a secondary victim to feel anger and helplessness, weariness from loss of sleep, deep sadness—even despair. As much as you care about the victim, you also have a right to your feelings. You just can't express them in a normal, open way. You, too, may need to talk and *diffuse* with a trusted *someone.* Through all of this, *Tiptoe.* Tiptoe carefully. Your role is one of listener and reflector. Yours is the role of constant friendship, no matter what. You can't make her leave, but you can be there when she does. Your love and strength will sustain her as you support her choice, but that choice has to be hers to make.

It's a difficult job being a friend of an abuse victim, but someone has to do it. They surely need a hand of friendship and support to be *lifted* out of this quagmire of confusion. But, just like any other *lifting,* you have to make sure that your feet are solidly grounded so that you don't *fall* with her. Make sure you have a strong and stable base by garnering support and help for yourself. Don't do this alone. Seek counseling from a professional through your local women's services. They know what to do and they know how to do it. Your job may be getting her safely there. Know that there is help in this for secondary victims, too. Seek it.

There is no need for you to dance alone.

# The Stories and
## *the Tellers*

Life and living afford each of us with a story. We all have one. Some go about their lives having told very little to others regarding their existence. Some live out their lives and then die having their life story written by others—after they are gone—in some biographical form. Some journal, write autobiographies or memoirs, opening their life's book to others as a way of inspiring and encouraging others to forge on when life becomes challenging. Stories of success are great for that.

*Telling* with a safe listener can calm and settle so much of the craziness that comes with abuse. When someone finds that what they are feeling relative to the craziness in their lives is normal, it is easier to calmly dissipate their troubles sensibly. They feel relief and even a bit liberated. They can even feel euphoric with a desire to help another. Service is a great way to turn your own troubles into a saving balm for another that is suffering. Oftentimes people come out of these trying situations wanting to help someone else that is suffering similarly so that another doesn't have to experience these traumas alone—or feel alone. This is why therapeutic groups are so successful in helping others feel supported.

The stories I am sharing are stories from the lives of individuals that want to do just that: help another. Not only are they seeking validation through telling their stories, but they also want to validate others and bring about understanding and compassion for those going through these challenges. *Telling* is powerful as stories and outcomes are *owned*.

So, let me introduce you to *the tellers*.

**Cammie** is a young mom. She had hope in a good marital choice that turned out to be everything but that.

**Kristy** is the mother of a daughter whose husband abused her. She chose to write her story in a poem entitled, *Dear Son-in-law*.

**Abbey** is also a young mom, like Cammie. She, too, tried to keep it together after many tries, having left and returned more times than she wished she had.

**Brenda** is the mother of a daughter that nearly died trying to leave her marriage. Brenda writes about the transformation in her thinking about victims of domestic violence.

**Lauren** has written a poem that she titled, *"Karma,"* desiring a little *poetic justice* for the abuse she endured.

**Karlee** has given her 24-year marriage a good shot and feels pretty lucky.

**Sara**, now a little older with young married children, chose to write her story of abuse from a *third-person* perspective. Her desire with her story is to share it with her children and grandchildren as not so much *her* story, but the story of *another* who found strength in herself through the love and support of her family—those that truly loved her.

**Dan** is a dad of four daughters. He shares a poem that his wife wrote for him after she gave birth to their oldest little girl about his soft *Daddy heart*. Dan shares his story of learning about his third daughter's abusive boyfriend.

**Michelle** is a young mother who shares her story of abuse and her personal triumph.

**Natalie** is no different than so many that get trapped in abusive relationships, hoping things will get better for her and for her kids.

**Becky** is the story of a daughter that was abused by her *perfect-on-the-outside* husband, written by her mother, *Becky*.

**We can do this** is a little sum-up of how we might identify in ourselves and others these behaviors that help, hurt, or harm. Selfless or Selfish behaviors are identified.

I am grateful for the generosity and courage of each of these *tellers*.

# Cammie

I never thought I would ever be a victim of a horrible crime. I am a relatively safe person. I was raised in a middle-class home in a safe suburban neighborhood. I have parents and siblings that love me. I haven't participated in what would be classified as risky behaviors of drug and alcohol abuse. I married a guy that was crazy about me; who told me he couldn't live without me. We were married in a church by a priest accompanied by *Pachelbel's Canon in D*. It was the perfect wedding. There were flowers, candles, a beautiful cake, and every promise of a wonderful future. Yet all of this did not keep me from being attacked by a criminal. The crime that happened to me happened within the walls of my own home at the hands of the man I hoped would love and protect me forever. It happened to me. I am a victim of domestic violence.

I am a survivor, but not without both the visible and invisible scars of what he did to me under the guise of a loving, dutiful husband. He was the perfect husband and we had the perfect marriage. *From the outside*. No one knew. He was good at keeping it all secret, and I was, too. But, it happened. The physical abuse was everything from slapping, kicking, grabbing, throwing, strangling, and his spitting (and *otherwise*) on me. The emotional abuse was much worse. He said every degrading thing imaginable. I was nothing—even less than nothing—without him.

It didn't happen all at once. It was gradual; just like boiling a frog. Things were good—*really good*—for a while. Then one time he got mad. This was different than his usual outbursts. This time he hit me. I was surprised at first. I didn't know what to think or say. I didn't know what to do. The next day, he apologized. He brought me flowers and cried when he told me how much he loved me. Of course, I forgave him. He was so sorry. I loved him. He was under a lot of pressure at school and at work. I was pregnant and things were stressful. Things got better—for a while. Then it happened again, just like the cycle of violence tells.

This went on for a few more years. I know you are wondering how I could stay with things being so bad like that. I wonder myself sometimes. All I can say is that I hoped things would get better. Things would be good; then things would be bad. Sometimes things were really good, and he was good to all of us. He bought me things, and he would take me on a trip that I had wanted. He'd be a good husband, and I would have hope that things were getting better, even the way I hoped they could always be. Then things would go sour for a while. I didn't know what to do. We'd usually have a blow-up, and he would leave saying something hurtful to me. He was so good at blaming me for what happened.

He'd leave for a few days or a week, saying he couldn't stand being around me. Then, he'd come back to see the girls and then tell me how pretty I was. I'd feel sorry for him and sorry for something I said or did that made him mad. We'd get back together for us and for the girls. Then it would happen again. It seemed with every bad time, the periods between the good and bad got shorter. With three adorable girls and a nice house, life looked good on the outside. The inside was everything but that. I wondered how much more and how much longer I could take it. I tried to leave a couple of times. I'd tell him that I was going with the girls to my parent's home, but when I started to go, he would promise to do better, so I stayed.

I tried so hard to make things better—to make things work —I really tried. Somehow none of it seemed to matter. After years of hearing how ugly, fat, useless, messed up, stupid, and what a poor excuse for a mother I was, it was, to me anyway, believable. I messed up his life, and he should never have married me. I was such a loser. Things got worse and worse to where I felt like even the girls believed it. I did. Everyone would do better if I was just gone. I wanted to go. I wanted to leave, but what would I do? Where would I go? How could I leave the girls? What could I reasonably do? Would everyone really be better off without me? I felt so crazy and confused. I wasn't a bad person but he had me believing that no one cared about me. I didn't have friends and I wasn't safe. Who could I tell and know that I was safe? Who really would believe me? It would be better for all of them if I was gone for good. I didn't know what to do. I was trapped and alone and so very frightened. Then, if I got up the courage and really did try to leave, he'd tell me that I couldn't. *What would people think?*

It is really hard to leave the outward perception—the *perfect-on-the-outside-looking-good-so-no-one-knows*-routine. They are so good at turning everything that is wrong about the marriage around on you. *How could I do that to him after all he's done for me and the girls?* After all, he's the smart one. He's the good-looking one. There are tons of women that would want what I've got. Everything is stacked on his side of the line. How am I, the stupidest, fattest, ugliest, and poorest excuse of a wife and mother going to make it without him? I was crazy. No police or lawyers would believe me over him. I'd lose everything. *Just try it.*

I have left out the ugly, the expletives, and the descriptives about the physical abuse because I want any reader—anyone—to be able to read my story. There was nothing glamorous or glorious about any of it. I don't want anyone to have those images. Not even me.

Then it happened. Our little seven-year-old daughter did something that absolutely flipped him out. It seemed as if I was watching myself as he did to her the same thing he'd done to me. It was a little thing, but in his rants and outbursts, it messed up his entire day. He completely lost it. He turned on me, then he started yelling at her and telling her she was just like me. I stood there—frozen—when I should have stopped him. I saw her take it, just like me. It was surreal. As I stood there not knowing what to do, he grabbed me hard and slapped me. I've taken slaps before this many times. This was different. I dropped to the floor. I couldn't focus, and I couldn't stand up. He grabbed me again, yelling for me to get up. My daughter was screaming for him to stop. He was yelling and hitting me over and over. Our twelve and fourteen-year-old daughters were in another room where they called my parents. My parents called the police.

The police came and took him away as he was trying to leave. It was all such a blur—the police and the questions, the ambulance, the blood from my mouth and my nose, my girls and the crying, my parents, my head was spinning, my ears were ringing. I couldn't think. I knew it was bad, and I knew things would be different, bad or worse. I didn't think any of it could get better—ever. He had left many times before, but now he was being taken away. He was gone. He was in jail, and a protective order was in place. I didn't know what would happen to us. I went home to live with my parents. In the process of all that was happening, the girls and I got some therapy and I started going to a group with women like me. It was good to know that I wasn't alone and that there was actually help that I could turn to. It was good for me and for the girls, too. We had help, and we were going to do better.

If you think this was the end of what was and the new beginning, think again. I re-thought that day so many, many times. I wanted to back it all out, say it didn't happen. *It was all my fault.* If I didn't, he wouldn't. I was so confused.

When our court date came up, there he was—all dressed up in a white shirt and tie. He smiled at me with his charming smile that I loved so much. How could I do this to him—to us? I wanted so much for things to work out for me and the girls. I wanted the good times. Was I doing the right thing? I didn't want this for us. I didn't want this for our family. I wanted the good part. I surely didn't want all of the bad. I knew I didn't want that. It was all so bizarre. I couldn't live like this, with all the confusion and the turmoil. Would he go back to all of that? What about my girls? What message was I sending them by staying? Would they end up with someone like him and even be someone like me? I couldn't do that. I remembered the women in the group—with the same hopes and the same confusion. I heard their stories and the manipulation, the believing and then the lies. Would that happen to me, too?

A thought came to me that struck me hard. It made me sick to even think about it. I knew that I couldn't live like this, but I honestly wondered if I would *die* like this. *I really thought I would die.* I really don't know what I would have done without the unconditional and dependable love and understanding of family and friends that literally picked me up and carried me to safety. I know where I would be. I would have died from his abuse or I would have ended things myself.

Victims of abuse leave the abuser an average of seven times before realizing that they need to leave for good. That's about what it took for me. I know it sounds so foolish, but I was caught in his cycle. When he was mean, he was really mean, but when he was nice, he was so nice that it gave me hope that maybe things would be like this forever. In my mind, I thought it was up to me. I was the problem. If I was nice, he'd be nice. It was me. I couldn't push those buttons in him. It was all up to me to make it better.

My family didn't know how to help me. I think a lot of it was trust. Each time I went back, they trusted my decisions less and less. I have since learned of the heartache and worries that my situation caused my parents, especially my mother. So, what would I tell the mother of a victim of abuse? I would tell her that your daughter needs you. She needs you more than anyone. She needs to know that you love her, even though she is married to or in a relationship with an abuser. Let her know that you are there for her and that you want her and her children to be safe. She needs to know that even though you made a poor choice—possibly many of them—that it doesn't matter. You are there. Your love will overpower any of the counterfeit love he is trying to confuse her with.

I would tell her mother to be patient with her! Be a constant of level-headed love. Don't allow yourself to get too involved, but encourage her to receive counseling, join a support group, and carefully suggest prayer and church attendance. It helps secure her spiritual base of who she is and really, who he is and what source of strength he turns to. It really helped me build my confidence in myself after the attack. Just remember that if you turn your back on her, she will be alone. He will continue to isolate her and the outcome will be grim. If you are there as a solid support with love and compassion, she will come to her senses eventually. She will realize your love for her, and she will begin again to love herself. Love is such a key element. He doesn't have that. No one who does these things can truly love another person. They love only themselves, but that really isn't love at all. *It's conceit.*

Closing that door behind me was a difficult thing to do. But, I had to do it. It has not been easy. And, it certainly isn't over —for any of us. But, I am out. I am starting over in a life that, for the most part, does not include him.

Love shouldn't hurt. The true and constant love of family and friends gets you through. I really had no idea how hard it was for all my friends and family to stand back and watch me go through this. They didn't know all of what was happening, but they knew something was wrong—terribly wrong. Yes, he had his "posse" and all of those that believed him. There was really nothing I could do about any of that. I am sorry about the loss of some friends and quite honestly, some family, too. But, I know who my friends and family really are. They have stuck by me and have loved me. I had no idea that there were so many people there to support me. I needed them. When I did finally leave, they were a fortress of strength for me. I couldn't have done it without them.

If you are thinking you need to leave, there is likely a reason for that. Get help. Find a safe listener. Tell someone. Go to your local women's shelter. If you don't think or know you are being abused, they can tell you. You are not alone. There is help. You can survive. No one needs to die trying.

# Kristy
## A poem from his mother-in-law

*Dear Son-in-law,*
*We trusted you.*
*We trusted your word, your vows, your promises—*
*Covenants.*
*So did she.*
*We trusted you.*
*You asked us for her hand.*
*We agreed,*
*Trusting yours would never hurt or harm;*
*Only protect.*
*We placed into your hand upon the day of your marriage,*
*Our most precious family commodity—*
*Our daughter.*
*Taking her hand in yours,*
*With our permission,*
*You passed through the loving all-protective wall*
*We built around her.*
*Nurtured over years of*
*Smiles and laughter,*
*Hugs and kisses,*
*Taught at her mother's knee and wrapped in her daddy's arms,*
*You promised to do as we—*

*To love, honor and cherish her above all else.*
*Above all.*
*Her and only her*
*Above all else.*
*All,*
*Even yourself.*
*We surrendered her to you—*
*Hand and all—*
*She, giving her heart to you,*
*Her heart, soul, her all,*
*Trusting you.*
*Vows, promises, covenants;*
*Hers*
*Firmly intact*
*As you,*
*Her trusted husband, guardian—sentinel—*
*Thoughtlessly, senselessly, carelessly, randomly—*
*Broke each.*
*Physically, emotionally,*
*Even most methodically,*
*You broke vows, promises—covenants.*
*You broke our trust*
*And hers.*
*More than this,*
*You broke her heart.*
*We trusted you.*

# Abbey

I am Abbey. I am the mother of three children—two girls and a boy—ages nine, seven and four, respectfully. They are good kids and I love being a mom to them. I love to sing, dance, sew, and I am really good at accounting. I nearly completed my Bachelor's degree in Accounting and Business before I got married. I got really good grades. I am a good person, and I have a lot to offer, given the opportunity. I am also a victim of an abusive husband. Let me tell you my story.

Jeff and I married when I was 21 and he was 24. He was charming and smart and seemed to have everything together. He was handsome. He was. He was amazing. How could I go wrong? And he was crazy about me. I knew it. He told me all the time. He even shouted it out to the world one time. Though awkward, I felt that it was true. I was so lucky.

Married life started out okay. It had all the elements of *Newlywedville*. I would say that the first two months or so went pretty well. Then he started picking at my appearance and the way I did things. He didn't like what I cooked. The first time this happened, it hurt my feelings. Of course, I thought maybe I needed some better recipes or maybe a new cookbook—something like that—it wasn't me. But then it continued, and he was less nice in his criticism. Then, over time, *I did* think it was me. I lost my desire to cook for him and then he would eat out more. He told me one time that an over-cooked burger was better than anything I was serving.

As far as my appearance, I'm not bad. Jeff called me, *"Gorgeous"* when we were dating. As married life got busy, maybe I didn't dress up enough or something, but I don't think I got worse looking. I didn't change that much, but whatever it was about me, it wasn't good enough. He compared me to supermodels and actresses. They were skinnier, had better figures or bra-sizes, better hair and eyes. He had his favorites. Then he compared me to my friends or his friend's wives or some *hot little thing* at his work. He got especially critical when I was pregnant. He commented one time that he was glad I couldn't fly anywhere because he'd have to pay for two seats for me; I was so big. *Really?* I hadn't gained that much at all! But he didn't stop there. He started to compare me to his friend's wife at work who was due about the same as me. She apparently looked fabulous pregnant, and he could see why she got pregnant. He told me he must have been drunk when I got pregnant. This really hurt my feelings. I didn't mean to look less attractive, but he made me feel that way. I didn't want to go out anywhere, and I certainly didn't want anyone to see me if I did.

I am smart. I know I am, even though he tells me I'm not. And I am friendly. I am a good friend. One thing I have noticed is that I have fewer friends that want to be around me since I married Jeff. He has been rude to my friends. He is so nice to everyone else, and so many people think he is great. But he treated my friends like they were a waste of time. It was embarrassing. I wondered why he wouldn't show them his friendly self. I wanted him to like them and them to like him, but he made things awkward for them. So, we didn't go out as couples anymore. I am not allowed friends unless he approves. Who will he approve of?

Maybe you are beginning to see what it is like to live with an abusive man. I can honestly say that it is like slowly dying inside. You lose the person you are in an effort to be the person he wants you to be, then he tells you that you aren't good enough. You can never win.

It's not like I chose to marry a mean and abusive guy. He was nice, even charming. He said nice things and treated me good. I got caught up in his attractiveness and his flattery. He's all about the outside, and that's all so important to him. I thought he was good because everyone was telling me that he was. So many other girls were jealous of me. It's hard for me to even think that before all of this happened I thought I was so lucky. In truth, he is narcissistic and arrogant. But at the same time, he is admired and well-liked by the outside world. Behind closed doors, he is manipulative, jealous, controlling, and mean.

People always ask why abused women stay. They wonder why they don't just divorce him and leave. I wish it were that easy. I am currently separated from my husband, but I have been with him for eleven years. This is the third time we have been separated. *Why have I stayed?* It has taken me six and a half years to finally realize that I have been psychologically abused. That's what allows them to physically abuse you. They get you thinking that you are so bad that you deserve everything they do to you. It just happens and then you don't know what to do about it. I knew the stuff he did was wrong—sort of. He got me so confused about me. These abusers have you so twisted and they are so convincing, you don't know if you are coming or going. They never take responsibility for their own actions. If they do something wrong, it is always your fault, even things that I didn't even know about. If I tell him that he's wrong, it just gets worse and then I'm stupid. It's almost better just to take it. What's the use of getting upset?

You are not allowed to have feelings. You're crazy, mental, you need major help. Let me give an example: Right before I separated from my husband, I got a phone bill in the mail that was over $300.00. As I was going through it trying to figure out why it was so much, I noticed some random calls at 12 am, 2 am 3, etc. I'm trained as an accountant. I am the one that has to balance our banking and pay the bills. I get in trouble if things aren't right. None of this seemed right. So, I called the number and it happened to be an ex-girlfriend I had heard him mention before. I confronted him about the calls without telling him that I already knew who it was. Right away, he said it was his boss. I told him, "Whatever. At 3 am?" And then I told him that I had called the number, and I had spoken to the girl. Why did he lie to me? I explained to him that it hurt me and if he did talk to an old girlfriend just tell me about it instead of lying and trying to hide it. He told me that if I was more trusting, then he could tell me the truth. He then told me they were just friends, and she was in trouble. She needed a friend and would I want him to turn his back on a friend? What kind of friend does that? Now, all of a sudden it was all about me!

Well, the next month when I got the phone bill it was higher than the previous month. I looked through it and I saw that same number again several times. There were other ones, too. I confronted him again. He told me he accidentally called it, but that I didn't need to question him. He couldn't believe that I trusted him so little that I would go through the bill again, and he wasn't going to be with a wife that didn't trust him and if I was going to keep pulling stuff like this, then he would go find someone who would trust him. This is totally typical of everyday life with an abusive husband.

How do you even work problems out? What do you say? You are helpless. When someone denies or won't even acknowledge something happened, what can you do? You are the one that ends up looking foolish. So, you shut down emotionally. Everything that happens is turned around on you and eventually you get so tired of hearing how wrong you are or how horrible, dumb, and stupid you are that you stop saying anything. It's just not worth another battle.

They take advantage of all that is good in you – your heart, your compassion, and your love. These men are really good at making you feel guilty. One time I went to pick up the kids from his house. We agreed that they could go to his house every other Saturday. He tried to talk to me about getting back together. I told him that I wasn't ready to reconcile. I just wasn't ready yet. Out came the waterworks. He is so good at turning it on to make me feel bad, and he does it right in front of the kids! He said that I just didn't realize how much he loved me. He would do anything to make me happy. He really just wanted a happy family. He knows he has done a lot of things wrong in the past, but that was the past and he regrets those mistakes ... etc., etc., etc. He has done this so many, many times before, and in the past, I have fallen for it because I wanted to believe him. Since he pulled all of this in front of the kids, I had to let him back because the kids were upset. He was the good guy. How are you going to divorce someone who is so sorry and so willing to do anything to save the marriage? I didn't buy into it this time, and I didn't react the way he wanted me to. I wouldn't play his game.

So, he started to try some new tactics. He started getting ugly and threatening. His classic phrase is, "So, you think you can play that game, do you? You have no idea what I can bring to the table." Well, I know what he can bring. He's mean, and whatever he can say or do is bad. If I didn't have kids, I would have been *so* out of there a long time ago! Having kids with an abusive husband adds to all of it a degree of difficulty. He will use the kids to hurt me. He will allow the kids to do things that he knows are wrong just to spite me. It's like he's thumbing his nose at me and all I thought that we, together, stood for. He buys the kids things that I say no to, but he doesn't help support them financially.

Money is always a battle. I can't do anything without it, but it is just one more battle, and I hate that I have to ask for it. Whenever he does give me money, it is a ridiculously small amount, yet he tells everyone in his family that I am trying to break him by begging for money all the time. He does this to hurt me. I am scared to go to court and ask for money. I know it sounds silly, but I am scared. I don't know what he will say. These men are predictable, yet so unpredictable. Their nastiness and meanness is like no other. They are going to get you back and get you back good for leaving them.

One night, after he had been really hurtful and mean to me, I realized that one of the reasons I have continued to stay around and continue to take it was because I was starting to believe what he was saying. I know I am not stupid, but I was

43

hearing it so much. I couldn't stand the horrible things he said about me and how mean it all was. I'm not at all what he says. I am the total opposite of what he has said, so I worked even harder, bent over backward a little more to try and convince him those things weren't true. I really am a good person, I really am nice. I really am smart. He is one of those controlling, emotional abusers. After years of hearing that you aren't like you think you are, they break you down to where you don't know anymore who you really are. It's like a wild ride with ups and downs and back and forths. You're trying to convince him that you're not what he says while he denies that he said anything like that and then you're trying to convince yourself that he really did say it while wishing that he didn't. You're so busy trying to stay ahead of it, that you don't know what to think or how to get out. They are master manipulators, and it is really hard to explain, but it is almost like they brainwash you to where you feel like you can't leave. You're too stupid. What would you do? They are stuck with you. You are stuck, too.

Being married to an abusive man is exhausting. I could go on for hours about what my husband has pulled and what I have had to put up with; however, I am still having a hard time making that final step and filing for divorce. Most of all I feel guilt—overwhelming guilt. I feel guilt for putting my children through all of this. I love being a mother, and it makes me so sick to think that they might be messed up and confused later on because of all that I have allowed them to see and hear. Will my son turn out like his dad? Will my girls marry someone like him? If they do, it is all because of me. All I have ever wanted was to have a good strong family and raise kind, obedient, well-rounded kids. I really want to get out, but I can't without making things worse. I want a fair, amicable divorce, but my husband won't let me have it. He is a narcissist, and he does not care about anyone but himself.

Narcissists don't care if they hurt their kids. I have had to learn that word and learn it well. A narcissist is someone that is overly preoccupied with themselves. They are the height of vanity, and they think everyone is in love with them. They think that they are the best at everything, and they are the most gifted and good-looking specimen God ever created. They are mentally unable to see how their destructive behaviors affect someone else because they can't see beyond themselves. They are totally and completely self-absorbed and self-centered.

Narcissists will use any avenue to hurt their victims, even if it involves using and manipulating the kids. The kids are caught in the middle and are their victims, too. These men will do anything if it helps their cause or fills their needs. I have often wondered how narcissists can do and say the things they do. They are just so unfeeling and cold. If you try to leave, they will make you look bad in front of the kids so that they are a victim of what you are choosing. The thought of my kids turning against me is almost more than I can bear. The abuser's scope of nastiness, control, and manipulation is out of most people's comprehension. They have no boundaries. They will use whatever means to get their desired goal. Someone told me that it will get worse before it gets better. I don't know if I have the strength or the stamina to keep up with all of this. It is a long, hard, and very daunting road. There is really nothing anyone can do to help me. I just have to get up the courage to leave—for good.

# Brenda

I was a Domestic Violence Snob.

Yes, that was me before we learned of our daughter's marital abuse.

I was smarter than that. *We* were smarter than that. Domestic violence happened to people that didn't know better than to get into a situation with someone that was mean. It happened to people that were less educated, less interactive, more dependent on the resources of another. It happened to people that were raised in a home where domestic violence was prevalent. Quite frankly, it happened to people that were different than me—than us. It happened to other people that didn't know better. I was—*we* were smarter than this. *We knew better.*

When our daughter called that night needing us to come and get her, we had no idea what she was really needing from us. She was living in another state. She was staying at a friend's house. She had run away—with the kids. We had no clue at all. She was running—running away from him—running from her husband.

When it all began to unfold, I was shocked. How could this have happened to her? How could she and we not have seen it before its beginnings? He had the perfect-good-guy image. How did we miss it? How did it happen right under our noses and we didn't see it? Now, what do we do? We were dumbfounded. How could this happen to her? How could *this* have happened to *us*?

When we began to realize what our daughter's coming home was really all about, we did all we could to keep her safe—to protect her from him. He was far away in another state, but his abuse was indelible in her heart. He had broken it. He had broken her. She was not the girl that she was before she married him. She was frail and unsure. She second-guessed her natural mothering instincts. She was confused, even lost when it came to natural decisions and situations. She had no decision-making skills, no

46

confidence, no hope or belief in anything good. She had no domain that she could claim as hers. He had taken every domain and ability away from her in his controlling and destructive conduct. He had wielded his hurtful and demeaning words, cutting her down with his threats and his abusive actions. He was hundreds of miles away and he still controlled her. His words beat her down and diminished her worth and she believed every one of them.

We couldn't get a protective order because he was so far away, and he was an upstanding citizen with no record of any wrongdoings. He didn't even have a speeding ticket. Yet, our daughter was terrified of him. He would find her. He would take the kids, and she wouldn't get them back.

Over the next weeks, we had to get a lawyer. We helped her file for divorce. Yes, we got that protective order one night when he came to the house and threatened her—and us. We had told her not to answer her phone when he threatened to hurt her. So, he came. We saw a side of him that although was very familiar to her, was so different than anything we had ever experienced. His anger and his volatile words have echoed in my ears ever since. We had loved him and supported him. We had supported their marriage and their family. How could any of this have happened – unnoticed by any of us?

Our daughter had guarded and protected her marriage from us because of all those things that we are now learning about domestic violence cycles and behaviors that are typical in such violent households.

How could this have happened to us? I don't have that answer exactly. I only know that it can happen to anyone. It doesn't matter who you are, how nice you are, how wealthy or poor you are. It doesn't matter what neighborhood or social circles you find yourselves in. Domestic violence has no face that depicts a race, a particular gender, sexual preference, cultural heritage, religious adherence, or belief system. The thing that is most frightening is that we are all so vulnerable because we, as a society, want to believe and see the best in people. Yes, I guess that sounds like I am a skeptic regarding the confidence we should have in humanity. Not completely. I still believe that people are inherently good—for the most part. I don't believe that my new view is tainted, darker or even skewed. It is clearer and less muddled up by my own preconceived stereotypes and lack of understanding. The rug was pulled out from under me—under us—and, I am more real now. I am more open now and more understanding now. This can happen to anyone no matter how smart you think you are.

I believe sincere truth more, and I judge situations I don't clearly understand far less. We are all just doing the best we can. We need to find ways to wrap our arms of love around each other and help each other rather than judge each other. We need help and support from each other to get through some of the messes we find ourselves in. Domestic violence and abuse can happen to anyone. It shouldn't, but it does. No one asks for it. No one deserves it. What we deserve is compassion, support, and understanding. We need considerate concern in eyes that don't see another's choices to fall into a trap such as this as foolish, but only see how they can help find a way to get the one that is trapped to safety. No judging. No criticizing. Just loving.

I was a domestic violence snob before this happened to us. I guess I've learned that we all have our little places of snobbiness whether it's being so athletic that you'll never be overweight, so rich that you'll never be poor, so wise that you'll never do anything foolish. Things happen that can change all of that so very quickly. Now I know that bad things can happen to anyone, even to those that know better. Things can happen. So, when someone asks what drives my passion in volunteering at the women's shelter, I have an answer. I know there are other girls like mine out there that are trapped in an ugly situation. They are broken-hearted. I choose awareness and change as my message of hope amid our experience of learning. I never want to be a *snob* of anything ever again.

# Karlee

Okay. I'm not exactly sure how to start.

No one asked me to do this. I actually asked if I could add my story here. I felt like I was pretty alone, but after reading the other stories, I know that I'm not. I, too am a victim of my husband's abuse. I want to call myself a survivor, but sometimes I feel like I'm just hanging on. Some days are better than others. I guess I'm *surviving*. I feel like things are getting better. I'm getting better at being single. I guess I can say that I'm lucky.

Our divorce has been final for just over a year. It's hard to think that something that was supposed to be perfect and seemed to be so beautiful in the beginning would end so ugly. We were married just short of 25 years. I remember so many times wondering if we'd make it to a landmark anniversary and then wondering why I was wondering that. It just seemed to me to be that place that solidified the rest of it. I guess I'll never know.

I know that for me it was about the kids, I mean, staying together. We have four of them. Two girls, two boys. They're great. They're beautiful. People have told me that so many times. Randy and I created some beautiful children together. They're good people, too. But, I have worried that hanging onto our marriage would leave them with a bad idea about marriage; that hanging on for so long would do more harm than good. I hate that they have seen what they've seen and heard what they've heard. But it hasn't all been bad. We've had some really good times. We really have. If you look at our family pictures, we look like a forever family. We look happy. I guess that's the biggest part of what I've hung onto. I've had hope that it would be good for them and for us. I had hope.

Okay. The hard part. He never hit me. Never. Never even once. I guess that's why I have been so confused about what really constituted domestic violence. I thought it was the violence part. I thought it was the hitting part that made it that. Sometimes I actually wished that he would hit me so that he'd get it over with—that I'd have a black eye or a fat lip that proved how hurtful he was to me. When I finally got into therapy, I was hit between the eyes with the concept that it doesn't have to be physically violent to be *violent*. Just this knowledge opened up my understanding of years of threats and hateful taunting. Randy wasn't like those *other guys*. He was better than that. His favorite phrase was, "You're so lucky ...." *Was I? Was I really?*

"You're so lucky that I have such self-control," he'd say.

"You're so lucky that I'm not like those guys that hit there wives, cuz I'd kill you."

"You're so lucky," he'd say as he'd storm out of the house, get in the car and drive away.

And, it wasn't just that, I mean—*his amazing ability to control his temper*— that made me so lucky. I was lucky he let me out of the house. I was lucky he didn't leave me. I was lucky he didn't run off with Suzy-so-and-so because she came onto him like so many other women did. *I was lucky that he was so faithful.* I was lucky until I found out that he wasn't faithful. He hadn't been. There were a lot of other things that he hadn't been so faithful about, too.

Well, I used his phrase—used his *"you're so lucky..."*— on him one morning. I'll never forget the fury in his eyes and the spewing of expletives and derogatory words that fired at me like a machine gun. I don't think I've been more terrified and petrified in my life. *Violence?* You better believe it.

51

There's so much more that really defines the end of what I thought would be perfect. The real truth in this is that *I really am lucky*. I'm lucky to have four good kids that are beginning to see the man that their dad really is— the man that I tried to protect them from. I'm lucky that I am free from the barrage of hurtful words that stung my heart and the threats of harm that kept me wondering when I'd be *unlucky*.

The good times? I guess I'm lucky there were enough of those that I'm not totally cynical about life and what a marriage could be. I'm lucky to have a future that though sometimes feels like I'm barely hanging in there, it's not threatening. It's doable. It's hopeful. I have me. I have my kids. I have friends and family. I have one day at a time. I'm pretty lucky.

# Lauren
## *Poetic Justice*
## *Karma*

*Karma – so that's her name.*
*She's new.*
*I hope she is everything you deserve.*
*Not long after you dumped me for someone else,*
*I suspected you'd find someone right away.*
*You did. You always did.*
*Coercing me to do things I never would have done,*
*Abusing me emotionally, physically and sexually,*
*You then drained my bank account for your own selfish needs,*
*Making me dependent on you for things that I needed.*
*Irony.*
*Then I had a baby—yours—for the record.*
*You called me "fat" as you porked on the pounds.*
*Mine came off in an eight-pound bundle. Yours remains.*
*You turned my friends and family into strangers*
*By your isolating insults and injury.*
*Yeah, I found the nasty texts and the fleshy pictures.*
*I've seen where you've been and the things you've done.*
*Each of your deeds will come back to bite you.*
*I promise.*
*You know what they say,*
*"What goes around, comes around."*
*So ... Karma ....*
*I think I'm gonna like her.*

# Sara

Sara was young. She was 15, barely a sophomore in high school when Devin started paying attention to her. According to the high school chatter, he liked 'em young. He was in and out of girls as quick as a car wash, and he always came out *cleaner*. At eighteen, Devin was tall, blonde and charming. He had graduated from City High the previous spring and now had a job painting and detailing cars. It paid better than most jobs available right out of high school. Money just seemed to come easily for Devin; he was smart that way. He'd grown up with a lot of it. His dad owned a large car dealership in town. The coolest set of wheels and the most expensive leather boots were his modes of transportation. They were his trademarks. He always dated the cutest girls. This was his trademark, too. Devin had it all. His sporty car and lavish gifts all spoke of success and entitlement. Sara was considered by some, pretty lucky. By others, she was only his latest victim.

It all looked great on the outside—like a dream—Sara remembers. She had it all so good. He was so nice and so cute. Sara recalled how he'd be right there in front of the school in his metallic blue Camaro. Devin was as hot and flashy as his license plate spelled out. *SWWWEET* seemed to be a license for more than his car. He was outwardly proud of all he had. He counted Sara as one of those assets. "I was it," she later mused. "I was part of his image."

Sara was kind, caring and considered a friend to so many. But now, very few of her friends were able to find time with her. Devin told her he needed her, and her friends were coming between them. He made an issue of any time Sara spent with her girlfriends from junior high. They were *squirrely and dumb*, he'd say, making fun of them. For a while, Sara defended them, but the more time she spent with him, the less her friends came around, and she lost interest in them.

"They didn't like him," Sara sighed. "He was mean to them." She recalled how her friends would try to talk to her at school and Devin would call them a name that made them feel foolish. Sara was embarrassed at first, then gradually her friends found other things to do that didn't include her, and Sara felt left out. She had outgrown them. After all, she was the one with the hot boyfriend. They were probably jealous, Sara had thought.

Over the next several months, Sara became very dependent on Devin. He was her security. She always had a ride home from school, a date to every dance, and really cool clothes. Devin had an eye for fashion and bought her something new to wear nearly every week.

"My parents didn't like it, but when I told him 'no,' he'd get mad," Sara noted. "I didn't want him to be mad at me. I didn't want to lose him."

She had to wear the clothes he bought the day after or she'd hear about it. He'd be mad at her. Devin had a temper. He didn't like being told "no." It upset him. He also didn't like any other guys paying attention to her. He wouldn't get really mad at first; just mad enough that Sara knew she had upset him. She would always apologize and beg back. He would assure her that he loved her so much that he didn't know if he could control himself if another guy started liking her. Sara seemed to feel oddly shielded by his defensiveness.

"How lucky I was," she remarked. "He was rich, cute, and crazy about me."

Sara's friends and family worried about her as her time with Devin increased.

"They were seeing changes in me that bothered them," she continued. "I was moody and less available. He was demanding. He was expecting so much more of me personally and physically."

They all told her that they didn't trust him and that they thought he was selfish and mean. Sara was taken by him. She'd have to break-up with him to be with her friends, and she knew he'd find someone else. She couldn't be a loser. He had so many girls that liked him. He'd have someone, and she would have no one.

Time at home was compromised and conflicts between Sara and her thirteen-year-old sister, Keri were becoming more and more frequent. Sara didn't do her chores, and Keri had to. Sara always had new clothes, and Keri wanted to wear them. But Steve, her ten-year-old brother, liked Devin. Devin was cool. Who else came to their house with a sweet car? Devin always had a pack of baseball cards with gum for him. As for Sara's parents, they weren't crazy about him, but they worried about saying too much. He confused them. Devin would bring Sara's mom desserts from the local bakery. If he was late bringing Sara home, who could complain? His gifts made them all feel awkward. He was polite enough sometimes that they wondered if maybe it was alright. Yet, they worried about the time Sara spent alone with him; his exclusive hold and his extravagant gifts. Sara assured them that he was good to her. They'd have lover's spats, as she would call them, and then he'd bring her flowers and take her out to a nice restaurant and even buy her a new outfit. Each time, he became progressively angrier, and each time she would apologize for making him mad. Without fail, every time, Sara recalled, Devin would promise not to get so mad again. He pleaded and begged. He justified his behavior, telling her that he just couldn't help himself because he loved her so much.

As the school year progressed, Devin became more and more demanding. He needed more time, more assurance of her love, more commitment. He wanted to marry her. He turned up the physical thermostat, and before long, Sara was expecting a baby. Her self-esteem became seriously compromised through rumors, the loss of close friends and the loss of the trust of her family. She had hurt and disappointed her parents. She was so ashamed. She had lost so much. Her dream of a beautiful church wedding was now diminished by the need for a quick and quiet ceremony. Sara's parents expected that Devin accept responsibility and do what was honorable.

A country club wedding had always been in Devin's mother's plans. They were disgraced by the pregnancy and agreed that a quiet ceremony would be best. Devin had been trapped by Sara and they were not happy. To save public face Devin's mother hosted the wedding in their home. This would be best. Sara's family was grateful and agreeable.

Sara was relieved to be married. No more secrets, no more excuses. They were now a family and she was his wife. She loved him and she would make him happy. She would be a good wife and mother. Sara would continue her high school education and prove to her new in-laws that she was smarter than they had thought. She would study hard and get through her GED program quickly.

Devin's parents helped them get a small house. Devin's job and his family's money provided a comfortable home for Sara and their daughter. She didn't need anything physical in the way of home and furnishings. Devin now worked for his father and made more money. Everything looked good on the outside. But things weren't as she remembered them when they were dating. Devin's control and demands seemed to intensify. He didn't like her hair. He wanted her to dress more seductively. He needed more expressions of her love, pressing her with more frequent physical expectations. He was mean sometimes and degrading to her in front of people. He made her feel foolish and dumb. Sara was doing all she could to prove to him that she really was smart. She was getting good grades and was in an honors class through a special Young Mothers program. There were assignments and projects to complete in this accelerated program and she wanted to do well. She was tired and stressed; worried and concerned. She was trying so hard to please everyone, especially him. She couldn't seem to do anything right according to him. Devin was increasingly short-tempered with her. He said unkind and insensitive things, calling her names in front of his family, belittling her. It hurt her feelings and broke her heart. Some days, she doubted he loved her at all.

Within the first year after the baby, Sara found herself pregnant again. Devin wasn't happy about this. He made comments to his friends that she had trapped him the first time, now she was trapping him again. He blamed her for her carelessness. His comments regarding her few extra pounds embarrassed her. He told her once that she looked like a porpoise and she was sickening to him. She was everything but the *cute little thing he had married*. Devin teased her about a new girl at his work that was paying attention to him. He was *Devin from Heaven* and he made sure Sara knew it. This girl wore things Sara could only dream of wearing. Devin bought Sara a piece of lingerie in a smaller size than hers. He expected a fit within three months after the baby. Devin told her she'd have to lose the weight or it was over. He'd find someone else who would fit into it.

A month before the birth of their son, Devin and a buddy from work decided to break off from the family car dealership to start one of their own. He hired the female co-worker and soon his work hours changed and he was home much less. Sara suspected an affair but felt trapped and afraid. She felt she was now on a shortened leash. As his own prediction would have it, rumors were swirling that Devin and his secretary were more than close business associates. He'd been seen with her in situations outside of the business. When Sara brought anything up, Devin turned things around on her, accusing her of ridiculous flirtations with strangers. Then he'd start on with hurtful comments regarding her dress size. It wasn't worth the fight. It was best to keep her mouth shut. She determined to lose the weight and gain control of the home-front. She graduated with honors from her high school program with two children under two. Her weight was now under control and she felt that she was back to her perky self. Sara's self-esteem was slowly on the rise with the help and support of her family. Devin seemed to be noticing her again; at least he wasn't calling her fat and ugly.

In-law relationships are oftentimes sensitive and difficult. Sara found that hers was no exception. Devin's mother dropped in without knocking often finding Sara and her house off-guard. His mother would comment about her hair needing attention and the baby being too skinny. Sara's daughter looked like her dad, his mother would chide. Lucky for Sara. But the baby's hair was too dark to be Devin's. Then it was on to the house. Sara's dishes and kitchen were prime for injurious commentary if anything was left in the sink. She couldn't seem to do anything right no matter how hard she tried. If she worked hard on the house, she was neglecting herself. If the house looked out-of-order, she was too worried about her appearance and not caring for the children as she should. She should be more like Devin's sister who was ten years older and a much better housekeeper. Sara decided to lock the front door and deal with Devin's mother's comments about her not wanting Grandma to come over and play with the babies. Sara couldn't dispute that.

With his business more demanding and stressful and his affair still under suspicion, Devin seemed to need some mental relief. His girlfriend was becoming difficult, and he decided to fire her. Sara confronted him about messages she had found on his phone, and he hesitantly admitted his little liaison. He swore that he had clearly broken things off. Sara was not surprised by his confession. Devin promised that he would never do it again and expressed that it was only because she had let herself go that he had found someone else. Sara was hurt but blamed herself, too. She'd work harder at sustaining her marriage. Things would get better now.

Things did get better but only for a short time. With two small kids and a demanding husband, Sara felt squeezed by all of the constraints on her time and energy. Incremental weight began to creep on. Devin not only noticed but commented regularly. He was back to the old routine. He called her fat and accused her of being obsessed with cookies. She was the original *Cookie Monster*. Sara was embarrassed and ashamed of her lack of physical control. He didn't gain weight as she did. She had to do something or she'd lose him again.

Time to do anything was practically out of the question. Getting out with two small children required serious planning, and Sara had little time for herself. Her mother would come twice a week so that they could go for a walk. They'd pack the kids in the stroller and walk for an hour. Sara confided once that Devin liked skinny girls, and she worried that she wasn't skinny enough. Her mother was worried. She questioned Sara regarding Devin's treatment of her. Sara wanted to tell more, but she was embarrassed. She didn't want her parents to think she wasn't happy. She really had everything she needed; a home, food, clothing, cute kids. Sara was trying to be a good wife. Maybe she needed to try harder.

Sara decided to join a gym she found that had childcare. She could take a few classes. Once again, Sara began to feel a little more in charge, and she had a new added bonus: friends. As a regular club member, she met other regulars. She now had girlfriends, some who had children that shared ages with hers. Sara had developed close ties with Chris and Anne, both young moms similar to herself. They started a playgroup where their kids could play together, while also sharing the clothes their kids had outgrown. After five years of marriage, Sara no longer felt so alone and isolated. Devin had moved her across town away from proximity to her mom and dad, and he made such a big deal about any time she spent with her sister and brother that he had alienated her whole family. Finally, with Chris and Anne, she had someone to talk to.

As Sara began to gain more confidence, it seemed to be Devin's job to keep her in check. He became increasingly more demoralizing. His physical thermostat was higher, and his demands amplified. Sara was to have the kids dressed, fed, and ready for bed by 7:30 when he came home. She was to be showered, made-up, and ready for him. He saw women all day, and if she wanted to keep him happy, she had to be ready.

Months had passed and Sara continued to go to the gym when she could. It was her turn for the playdate at her house. Devin unexpectedly came home to get some things for work. She introduced him to Chris and Anne. Devin was polite and very congenial. He had a great enamoring public presence. People liked him. Her friends thought he was really nice. Sara felt good about him meeting her friends.

Later that evening when Devin came home, Sara thanked him for being so nice to her friends. She thought maybe they could get together as couples, with their husbands and do something. Devin was outraged. How dare she think that her little friends and their college-student-husbands would have anything in common? He had his own network of friends that didn't include her or them as a couple. His friend's wives were babes, and he was too embarrassed to take her out with them. She was lucky that he would let her out of the house by herself. He told her that her friends would find out in time how weak and stupid she was and dump her like everyone else. He made sexual comments about Chris. He said she came on to him. Sara couldn't imagine that Chris had done that. What had he seen that she didn't? How could she ever trust Chris now? Devin, in his careful and calculated way, had placed paranoia exactly where he wanted it. Sara became less trusting of her friends and began finding fault in them herself. Any comments they made, she saw as potentially hurtful and unkind. Her friendships decreased. Her time at the gym, terminated.

After seven years of an up and down marriage, Sara found herself pregnant again. She had lost twenty pounds by her own determination and had started babysitting a few children after school. She was feeling good about herself. She had some money that she could call her own, and she no longer had to beg Devin for what she felt she needed. There had been a need for parent helpers at her children's classrooms and with soccer, dance, and gymnastics, Sara's days were full. She enjoyed being busy and involved. But, another baby would certainly change things. Devin was still gone quite a bit, but he seemed to be more settled in their marriage. Devin's sister was now divorced and his mother spent more time over there. This was good. Sara's parents became involved more in their lives as she felt her kids needed their grandparents. She needed them, too. Her parents suggested church attendance for Sara and the kids. She had wanted to go back to church again. She had been raised in a Christian family, and she felt that her children needed to have this element of faith in their lives. Things were feeling good again.

Adding Sunday church service attendance to their lives brought a new challenge Sara wasn't prepared for. Devin told her that he thought church would be good for all of them. He'd come, too. Sara felt confident that this would bring a change of heart and more love to their family. For a couple of months, she was right. Church attendance was going pretty well. They all seemed to enjoy it, that is until Devin had a disagreement with the church leadership. He declared to Sara one day that he was done going to church—loud and clear. He boldly declared that he was better than the whole lot of them. Why should he spend his Sunday—his day of rest and leisure—with a bunch of hypocrites? From then on out, each Sunday was a day of contention and criticism. Now, Sara was a hypocrite along with her new church friends and her family.

Early in their marriage, Sara had known that Devin liked to drink with his buddies. He didn't do it very often that she knew of. She didn't like it, but she didn't dare complain about it. She didn't want to make it an issue. It seemed that now he was drinking more and staying away from home more. When he did come home, he was late, boasting excuses that included some buxom beauty that he took a test drive with or how he was trying to decide about whether or not to leave her. Nine years had passed, and their three kids not only noticed things were wrong, but now they were part of it. Devin yelled more, and he was becoming more physically hurtful. He clearly had a drinking problem. His infidelity was always an issue, but one Sara was scared to even know about. He no longer waited for the kids to be out of the room. He was showing more of his anger towards Sara in front of them. There were few restraints in his threats to her. He regularly told them how fat and ugly their mom was compared to their friend's moms. He made fun of her meals and would throw her dinners in the trash, telling them to do the same. It seemed like a game for him as he'd take the kids out for pizza or burgers as a reward for not throwing up their dinner. Things were getting worse and worse. Sara's self-esteem was so diminished that all she could do was get through each day. How could she leave? She'd spent the last ten years defending and making excuses for him. Her parents had warned her about him. So had her friends. Why hadn't she listened to them? She was stuck. Sara felt that the kids thought she was dumb and worthless as a mom. That's what Devin would tell them. She made him sick. Fat and ugly, though she weighed less than she had in years, her mental image was depicted in every threat Devin dealt her. In her mind she was useless and a burden to all of them. He validated every hateful thing by telling her everyone agreed with him. She was easily replaceable.

Sara was frustrated. How could she get out? Where would she go? Her in-laws treated her indignantly. Her parents were busy with work and their own lives. They knew her marriage had troubles, but how could she tell them how truly awful it was? It was all her choice. She got involved with him against their better judgment. She's the one that had gotten pregnant. She was stupid. Now she had three kids who thought she was stupid, too. Did any of them even want her? What good was she?

63

One day, Sara had taken just about all she could. She informed Devin that she was going to run away. She told him that he couldn't hurt her if she was gone. He mocked her with his, *then what?* Where would she go and who would ever want her? He told her she had too much baggage. He was stuck with her, but he had women lined up as soon as she was gone. The more she thought of the life she had chosen, the fewer options she could see in a future for herself. Sara's family was worried and counseled her to seek help through her clergy. She went one time and was counseled to bring her husband in with her. He wouldn't come. She was the problem, not him, he'd say. She was a nutcase who needed an exorcist. She couldn't stay with Devin one more day. But, really, where would she go? Who would have her?

In the days that followed, Devin became more hurtful and violent. He would grab her, push her, and hit her. One night he came home to find the kids still awake. He grabbed her and threw her down in front of them. She wanted to die and wished he had killed her. She was fat, lazy, and a poor excuse for a mother. She was a lousy wife. She couldn't do anything right. No one liked her. Certainly, no one loved her. Her children didn't love her; she was a burden to her family. That night, with a bottle of sleeping pills, Sara determined that everyone would be better off without her. She took what was left in the bottle and fell asleep. It would all be over by morning.

Light broke through the window of Sara's room. She woke up the next morning past her usual wake-up time wondering why she had survived. Devin was right. She couldn't do anything without botching it up. Her mother called and immediately came over. Sara was desperate, feeling unloved and unwanted.

With the help of her parents, Sara moved back to their home with her children. She began seeing a therapist. This was helping her. She trusted him to listen to her. Still, Sara had to deal with Devin regarding the kids. He was so up and down all the time. He wouldn't pay any attention to them for a week and then he'd call and say that he was taking them to Disneyland or the race track for the day. Then she had to hear from the kids what a great dad he was. He didn't want them necessarily. He just wanted control of them. It seemed to her that he liked his freedom to do as he chose; drinking, coming home late, and being with other women. As far as being a dad, he used them to get back at her. He wanted the freedom and the ability to wow 'em without the responsibility of raising them. Was she the only one who could see that? He wanted it all his way. Being a full-time dad would only complicate that. He wanted to control them like he controlled her.

Devin was a head-gamer. Sara wouldn't see or hear anything for several days, and then out of the blue, he would do something nice and confuse her. He would tell her he missed her; he loved her and needed her. He'd take her and the kids to a movie, telling them, in front of her that she had hurt his feelings. He'd tell them he wanted them to be a family again. The kids would beg her to go back to him. Devin knew how to manipulate and play with her heart. Sara would think that maybe she could give him another chance—for the kids. She'd go back for a while and then something would happen that made her feel unsafe again. It didn't take long for him to be his regular self: mean and humiliating. After so many difficult and hurtful trial resolutions with Devin, her therapist asked her one day, "When is enough *enough*?"

Through counseling, and over time, Sara was able to discard many of her feelings of despair and replace them with hope. She wanted a divorce. She didn't want to play his games anymore. She wanted the marriage to be over. Devin laughed when she told him. He said that he had just taken his name off of their accounts. According to the bank, he didn't have any money. She had more than he did. The car business wasn't doing very well, so he only reported losses on their taxes. She'd get nothing. Good luck, he told her. Sara knew nothing about the business. Was he lying? She thought they were okay financially. She didn't know what to do. He was so good at confusing her. Now he'd never take her back, and what would she do? She had made such a mistake and had messed up her life and everyone else's. They'd all be better off without her. After one more attempt at taking her life, her parents intervened. They took her and the kids to their home to stay.

Not long after, Sara looked at her daughter who had just turned fifteen. She was a lovely girl and boys were noticing her. How could she protect and keep her daughter from making the same mistakes she did? She persevered, filed for divorce, and moved on as a single mother. She realized that being single had to be better than the life she was living married to an unfaithful, controlling, hurtful, and dishonest man. She wanted to show her daughter an example of strength and courage rather than fear and despair.

Enough *was* enough. Over time, and with the love and support of her family and friends, she gained new courage and the strength to make a new start. Feeling there was a reason she had awakened from that first and even the second attempt at herself, she determined to get herself back. Sara's battle was not over. She had many setbacks due to Devin's manipulation and deceit. It was very difficult. The road was not easy, but after three years, Sara did meet a man who was thoughtful and trustworthy. He, too, had been hurt in marriage. He proved to be a kind and understanding man. Spence was everything Sara hoped Devin would be.

As for Devin, he quickly remarried and over those same three years, had divorced two more times. He became increasingly more absent and less attentive as a parent. The children struggled from time to time. He would play them and confuse them with his lavish gifts, making up for his parental forgetfulness. He proved himself to be as he always had been: undependable. Most often he had trouble keeping commitments he had made with each of them. He didn't come when he said.

He didn't do what he planned, and his drinking and parties were immature and frightening for them. They didn't like being with him. His joint custodial requirements and child support conditions clearly showed him to be irresponsible and flaky at best. Sara's children eventually came to see their mother as truly good and kind. Her love had never failed them. They saw Spence as one who led and supported their mother and them. He was not their dad, and they all knew it. He was better than simply biological. He loved them. He loved her. He listened to and protected her. Now, Sara is stronger, and she has found that life outside of Devin—*and completely void of him*—can be happy. *Very happy.*

Fortunately, Sara's story has gone from tragic and disparaging to being a story on its way to a very happy ending. Life for Sara hasn't always been blissful, but she now says that she knows what "happily married" looks and feels like. Life has its challenges, but her marriage isn't one of them. She still has to deal with Devin when family issues arise. She still has to see his family and deal with their unkindness and judgments from time to time. It's all part of her life. But, Sara worries less and has learned to ignore Devin's hurtful comments and attempts at manipulating and controlling her. Sara marks herself as lucky. This story could have had a very tragic ending. Her heart had been seriously broken. Devin's destructive words and heartless abuse nearly killed her. Sara is a survivor and no longer a victim of Devin from (other than) Heaven.

# Dan

*Dad of an abuse victim*

*My baby girl.*
*Sweetly, softly sleeping upon my chest;*
*Our hearts together—beating;*
*Mine, melting.*
*I, her Daddy;*
*Little fingers tightly wrapped around mine*
*Or is it me around hers?*
*Already.*

Yep, that was me. Each time the doctor passed that new little bundle of pink into my arms, there I was, again, in love. These little girls melted my heart. It's not an easy thing being the dad of daughters. You have to be the-man-of-the-house: a tough guy, a man role model with a rugged exterior. But, also soft on the inside. I've had to learn about Barbies, sparkles, and the latest teen-aged girl's book series. We have four of them—I mean, daughters. Four beautiful girls with their own individual personalities. I wouldn't want it any other way.

I learned how to curl hair, paint toenails, and listen to boy bands. When my wife had to work, I had to pick up the hair-do detail. They like looking pretty. I like it too, I guess. They are lovely girls. I hear people talk about my girls and how cute and pretty they are. There's an image in that, and I've been party to all of the *keeping it up*. I've also been the tough guy with the threat of a purported shotgun when their dates were coming around. They knew I would never really use it or really, seriously, even think about it. Well, until one day.

Our third daughter, Rose, was dating a kid that was just a little edgy—you know—the bad-boy kinda guy. I can't say that

68

I didn't see a little of myself in him, but then again, no. I wasn't like him, and he wasn't me. I guess we were both dumb teenage guys, but there was something different about him. He pushed my buttons. From a distance—if you looked at the whole package—he seemed like an okay kid, but there were notable little things that bugged me about him.

Drew was his name. He played rugby on the high school team. He was cocky; kind of a smart-aleck. He had a little beard—a goat patch. Even though the rugby coach had required that the boys shave, he didn't. He had the attitude that the coach would have to go ahead and cut him. Then what would the coach do? His team would lose without him. He was a flanker—the open side. I have to say that athletically he was good. He knew the game. He got the job done. But, I'm not too sure if his teammates liked him off the field. That, right there, says a lot.

Well, Rose liked him. At first, it seemed like a crush and some little fling that would blow over. But, it didn't. It got more serious and more committed as time went on. She'd come home late after our designated curfew. I didn't get mad. I just reminded Rose that she needed to get in on time. I'm a dad. I'm the rule enforcer and I'm "the softy." It's a delicate balance. I wasn't around that much to notice some of what was happening, but when the other girls— her sisters—commented about him and how he treated them, I wondered. They didn't like him. My wife had expressed a few times that Rose would have come home crying or that she had come home to change her clothes mid being with him. Weird, I thought. But this wasn't the only odd thing. Rose had changed her hair color. Not an overly strange thing for kids nowadays, but it was for her. She had lost weight, too. Sure, she looked thinner, not too unhealthy, but she didn't need to. Just odd.

This was the beginning of what took months to finally unravel. He controlled every decision she made from makeup to meal choices and who she would be with and have friendships with. As long as she did what he said, everything went well. Drew had her doing school assignments, making his lunch, cleaning his car, and who knows what else. He had manipulated her to think that she was nothing without him. She was lucky to be his because he was so great and so important.

If I could put my finger on one thing—one time—that things started to click for me, I'd map it to the time she came home really late. I mean really. We were starting to get worried— 911-worried. Rose had left in a rush. Drew was waiting for her out in his car. He was getting lazy with her—he didn't come to the door anymore. He'd text her when he wanted her to come out. He just sat and waited in his car. I commented to Rose that he needed to come to the door. She brushed it off saying that he was in a hurry. He was always in a hurry. She didn't want to make him wait. Well, I was going out to talk to him. He could wait.

Rose knew I was coming. Her "Daddy—don't!" made me both suspicious and determined to do whatever it was that she was afraid I was going to do. I was going to remind Drew-Rugby Star that even though he thought he was tough, I was tougher. I saw something odd coming from a handbag that Rose was carrying. It looked like a shirt that I knew belonged to Rose. Why would she need a shirt in a bag? What was going on?

As I approached Drew's car, Rose became agitated. I said to Drew, "How come you don't come to my door anymore? Ya' scared of me?" I chided. He laughed. It wasn't a hearty laugh or a *you're-funny* laugh. It was an *in-your-face* laugh. What was that all about? How did I deserve that?

So, I was not finished here. Yeah, Drew was in a hurry, alright. He had my daughter, and I was challenging him. So, I continued. "Drew," I teased (in his face), "I've been missing ya, Buddy."

I looked at Rose. She wouldn't look at me. I spotted the bag. "What's in the bag, Rose?" I asked.

"We have to go, Daddy," she said. She never did look up at me.

Drew backed the car out of the driveway. I watched him drive away.

He wasn't doing anything illegal. Just illogical, arrogant, and condescending. I asked my two daughters that were home what they had seen in all of this. Ruby said that Drew was a jerk. Randi confirmed that. I asked about the shirt. Had they seen it? What was going on? Randi said that Rose had mentioned to her one time that he didn't like her clothes. When they went out, he would decide what she would wear. She had to bring a change of clothes in case he disapproved. What else was he doing? What else was he controlling? Was that why she lost weight? And her hair color. Did he choose that, too?

That night Rose hadn't come home and it was past her curfew. I was waiting. I was worried, too. I didn't trust Drew one bit. As worried as I was, I had 911 positioned on my phone, and I was ready. It got later, and I was more worried. I prayed like I had never prayed before. Had I said too much? Had I pushed too hard? What would he do to secure his control of her? Had I messed up in my *back-at-him* in front of Rose? Would she protect him, defend him? Would she defend me? Not likely. Would she even come home?

As the hours progressed, I sat in the dark where lights from cars from any direction wouldn't disclose my whereabouts. Anxiety and worry were beginning to lose out to my weariness and exhaustion. When I thought of Drew with my daughter this late, I was glad I had my shotgun—just for good company. Suddenly, I heard the motor of a car—his I was sure—come up the hill. It was almost three in the morning. Where had they been? What had he done to her? *What would I do to him?*

The silence of the night was broken by obscenities and the driver's side door opening, then slamming closed. More obscenities and the passenger door flew open. He grabbed my daughter by the arm and yanked her out of the car. I was up out of my spot—my shotgun by my side—but then, I paused to watch what would happen next. Drew seemed to be looking my direction. He must have heard something. Not seeing me, he called Rose a few names, and from what I could see and hear, he shoved her. I grabbed my gun, but I saw her get up and crawl away. I came out from my darkness as a presence with my shotgun in hand. Drew saw me coming. And I was. He quickly got in his car and drove away.

That night, in the darkness, Rose told me of Drew's weeks of pressing her for nude photos. She had resisted. That night, he had told her that he hated what she was wearing. He had taken her to a park where he wanted her to change her clothes in front of him. He wanted a picture. She refused. He had been drinking and had been vulgar and demanding. He became aggressive, grabbing her purse and her things. His phone was in the console when he knocked it down by her feet. In his distraction, she grabbed it and put it in her pocket. He demanded that she undress for some pictures. He wouldn't let her leave the park until he had gotten a picture on his phone. She ran from him and found a place to hide. Her phone was in her purse in the car, but she had his. Rose watched as he searched for his phone in the car. She saw him get out and look for her. Then she saw him enter the park restroom. Rose turned off his phone and threw it into some bushes.

When Drew came out of the restroom, there she was. She knew if she ran, he would hurt her, so she told him she was sorry, and she wanted to go home. All he could think about was where he had left his phone. Thinking he had left it at the gas station earlier, he drove Rose home so that he could search for his phone. He was angry, calling her names and accusing her of lying and cheating on him, but he did take her home. He had taken her phone from her purse and couldn't use it because of the passcode. She refused to give it to him. That's when they came to our house. And that's when he had grabbed her, pulling her out of his car.

After sorting a few other things out, Rose and I called the police, telling them all that had happened. They located the phone and found it to be filled with nude photos of several of her classmates, among others. I am grateful that our story has, what I would call, a happy ending. I am grateful that I never raised my gun, though God knows I thought about it. I have my daughter, and she's safe. We all learned some lessons in this. She knows that I would do anything to keep her safe. I know that I have little power when it comes to raising daughters. But, I am their dad. I do know I love them and their mother and just like they are this "Daddy's Girls," I am my girl's daddy. My girls still and will always have me wrapped around their fingers.

# Michelle

I feel like my story is so unique because it's my story, but when I hear about others, it almost seems like abusers have their own coded handbook of how to treat women and get what they want. I got sucked into all of it. It didn't happen all at once, but I was trapped before I knew it. He was charming and witty and sweet. When I look back, I can see how it all happened. He wasn't mean in the beginning. It was subtle and incremental—I guess. Just when I was getting comfortable, he turned up the heat, and I couldn't figure out how to get out of it. This is my story.

I actually grew up in an abusive home, and I vowed that this would never happen to me. I had seen my mom get beat up, and I was going to have a different life than this.

I was almost 18 when I met him. Don was 24. He was so good-looking and so smooth-talking. He called me *babe* in front of my friends. He would come to my school to pick me up. He'd take me to work and pick me up. My mom and step-dad thought it was great that I had a ride everywhere. He was always around. I was his everything. That's what I thought, anyway.

The first few months of our relationship was just as I had hoped it would be. Don and I were in love. We were together all the time. If he was at his work, he'd call me, always wanting to know what I was doing. I'd tell him I was thinking about him because I was. He made sure he was all I thought about because he didn't let me do anything with my friends. I thought he loved me because he was always there. I didn't know his game. I didn't realize that his stalking and his jealousy was that thing that was behind all of that. I thought it was because he loved me. Sometimes it was kind of smothery, but then, sometimes it was great to feel so together with someone. I did have to be careful, though. If he saw me talking to another guy, he would get crazy.

Don was smart. Not so much book smart, but he knew a lot of things like how to make things and fix stuff. He was good with his hands. He liked working on cars and machinery. He was also good at arguing. I saw him get after some kid at his work and make him look real stupid. He was good at turning things around. He did it to me, too, blaming me for something that I didn't say or do and using my own words against me. It was gradual. But when it started it just kept happening more and more. I really wasn't prepared when it happened the first time—the physical stuff. It was out of nowhere. First, he hit me. He hit me across my face and my neck. Then he said that he was just doing what I wanted. He reminded me that I had told him once that I loved him because he was strong, and he knew what was best for me. *What?* Yeah, I loved that Don was strong. I think a lot of women like men that are strong so that they can protect them; not bust their jaw. So, I had told him one time when he was kissing me that he was a good kisser. I told him that he knew the best way to kiss me. I regret that I ever said anything to him.

As far as Don hitting me, it didn't happen that often—at first—and he was always sorry. He'd get jealous or he'd think I was flirting with the guy that helped me at the self-checkout. I just had to be careful. Being with Don was really good sometimes and really not so good, too. The good times usually followed a bad time, so I was starting to get used to the pattern. I felt like I just had to figure out how to have less and less bad times. Whatever I had to do, I would do it.

So, we were still together and still in love and people in love get pregnant. Yep. I was pregnant about a year into our relationship. He didn't like me being pregnant. He called me *fat*, but I wasn't that bad. I thought he just didn't know what to say about it. So, I had an adorable little boy, and I was so happy. He looked so much like Don that we called him, Donny. Sometimes he was a good dad—I mean around his family. He seemed proud of me and Donny when we were around his family, but in other places, I wasn't so sure. There were times when Don seemed pretty indifferent about the whole thing. As Donny got a few months older, he wouldn't even *bond* with him as a dad should. I thought maybe he was just scared or worried. He was good with his brother's two kids. They were older. It might take some time.

Well, time came and went. He didn't get up to help and he refused to change diapers. Don said to me one day, "Women are made to do that stuff."

Diapers? What was he talking about? Then, one day, out of nowhere, I was holding Donny. I had actually just finished feeding him. Don called me a slew of awful names and accused me of sleeping around. He said Donny wasn't his. How could he say all of that? He knew I was faithful to him. I never left his sight! The thing that worried me was that I was holding Donny. I got mad and let him know it. He grabbed my hair and twisted it tightly. He snapped my neck really hard. I fell down. He didn't seem to even care that he could have hurt him, too. So, then Don left for a few hours and came back late that night. He said that it's all because he loves me so much that he acts like that. He said he was worried that he wasn't as important as the baby. I got sucked back in.

So, we had this neighbor in our apartment complex that thought he knew me. He was nice. After talking, I found out that he went to school with my sister. I look a lot like her. It was funny. We had her in common. His name was Todd. Todd was gay. I mean, he had no interest in me, but he was friendly, and he was cute with Donny. Todd was cool, and I liked him.

Don didn't like that I talked to Todd. Just like any time I was around some random guy, he'd ask what his name was and where he lived. He started going at me about Todd. I laughed. Todd was my friend—just a friend. He wasn't interested in me. Don said some mean things. I told him to leave Todd alone. He wouldn't stop. He said that he was going to hurt Todd if he saw me talking to him again. I didn't want Todd to get hurt for just being my friend. So, I stopped talking to him—at least when

Don was around. I just had to make sure I wasn't around him where Don could see him.

Things would be good, and then it would get bad, then worse, then good again. It seemed when I would be ready to call it quits, Don would be so sorry. He loved me and he was just having stress at work, or he was worried about me leaving—that was a twist. He'd hit me because he thought I would leave him? I'd stay for all kinds of reasons. Don was loud sometimes when he'd get mad. We had a neighbor that had called the cops a few times when she'd hear fighting. They'd come over, and I'd tell them it was my fault. I got a citation once because the cop said someone had to be accountable. I seemed to be willing to take all the blame. I had to go to court, and I was ordered to do anger management. Me! It was humiliating. I hated that lady for doing that to me. Now, I know she was really only trying to help me. I wasn't helping myself by taking the blame.

So, the neighbor lady called the cops again after Don got drunk and was yelling again. Don was so mad. He was going to take her on one day. Well, he threatened her and got in her face. He said all he did was touch the top of her arm, but her kid called the cops. Don got a citation and had to go to court. Now it was him doing the anger management. We moved to another apartment after that.

We were at the new place when things started getting bad again. Like life goes, I was pregnant again. Donny was three now, and I was trying to potty train. It was just so hard. Don didn't like any of this. He didn't get mad at Donny, but he sure got mad at me if there was an accident. This one night, Don had been drinking. He was asleep when I brought Donny in to sleep in our bed because I was too tired to stay up and take care of him. It was easier. Donny peed the bed close to Don and Don woke up. He went crazy. He grabbed me by the hair and threw me on the floor. I got up and grabbed Donny. I worried that Don would hurt him this time. I was eight months pregnant and I fell hard on the floor. I stumbled down the hall with Donny in my arms. All the while, Don was yelling and swearing at me, kicking and hitting me. Donny was screaming because he was so scared. Don went to hit me and cuffed Donny right in the ear. I got us into the bathroom and locked the door. Don was pounding on it. I told him I had to bathe Donny and to go back to bed. He yelled some more stuff and went back to bed.

As I sat in the bathroom thinking, I realized we were in a bad situation, little Donny and me. I dreaded coming out. I was having a baby—a girl. Did I want this for us? Did I want this for her? I knew what life was like as a little girl, and now I knew what my own mom went through. I sat there and thought about a time when a cop had come over to our house for like the third time and he said to me as he was getting ready to leave, "You must like this because you haven't left him yet."

It made me mad at the time, but at that moment in the bathroom, I was seeing me as he did. If I didn't like this, I would leave. I must like it. I didn't, so I had to make a change for me, Donny, and my daughter. I waited until Don left for work and called the cops to come and get me. I wanted to leave. I was taken to the crisis shelter and we ended up at the hospital. My bruises and Donny's perforated eardrum were injury enough for Don to be charged with assault on me and on Donny. He went to jail. There was no question what he did. I even had the support of the cops that had come to my house. Though this wasn't exactly the end, it was a beginning. I am now in school studying to be a nurse with the help of so many people. Don didn't want custody. He didn't want to have to deal with me. I was lucky in that way. He was on to someone else, and I didn't want him in my life or my kids' lives. It was hard, but living like that under his control and abuse day to day, was harder and so much worse. I can do this for me and my kids. I can change my life story to be better for all of us. And I have.

# Natalie

I haven't told many people about all that happened. Sometimes all it takes is closing my eyes to have it all come back. My story doesn't seem that different than too many others that I have heard in group. He didn't start off being mean. Can you imagine being smacked across the face on the first date? You'd run and call the police. Five years and two kids later, that was the last thing on my mind. Surviving and keeping my kids safe was my constant thought process.

I can think back on the time when I knew things weren't good. Marty drank. I did, too, when we first got together, but after a while, I realized that one of us had to have our head on straight. I was pregnant, and that made it so I quit drinking. I was so sick of the smell and the way it made me feel—it was an easy thing to quit, for me anyway.

So, he'd get with his friends from work, and they'd go out and drink and he'd come home late. After you stop drinking, you realize how irresponsible and reckless all of it is. I worried that he'd be driving. I worried that he'd be drunk and hungover the next day and then couldn't go to work. I worried that he'd be angry. Sometimes my sister, Deidra, would come over. He didn't like her, and she felt the same about him. It would make him mad when she was at our house. He'd be even *madder* if I wasn't home when he came home. I had to be home or he said he'd come looking for me. He always figured that if I wasn't home, I was likely with her. That was my life. It wasn't all like that, but it sure felt like it sometimes. Marty drunk or mad and me trying to stay out of his way.

One night—we'd been together about a year—Marty came home and Deidra was still there. She was just leaving. We were crocheting some potholders for her to sell at the swap meet and watching a movie. He was drunk. Deidra was heading out the door when she made a comment about his drinking and driving and making the world unsafe or something like that. He did what he normally does, calling her a name with a cuss word attached. She, of course, told him what she thought of that and she told me she'd call me when he wasn't around. I felt like a referee. She was right. He was wrong. I knew it. She left, and Marty gave it to me for helping her. I got defensive and told him she was my little sister and he needed to knock it off. *Knock it off?* He blasted me in the face with his beer-breath. I told him to go cool off. He was drunk. I thought he was sitting down when instead of sitting, he grabbed the wooden chair and hit me in the back with it. I was shocked. I think my jaw was hanging out when he swung hard and hit me in the mouth. I fell to the floor and held my bleeding mouth. He went into the bedroom, and I stayed on the couch. I didn't sleep. My back was so sore and my mouth. I couldn't believe what had happened.

The next morning when he saw my fat, split lip, he knelt down beside me on the couch and cried. He begged me to forgive him and promised to never hit me again. He wouldn't have done it if Deidra hadn't been there. She got under his skin, he said. I was stunned. But, I'd never seen him so mad, *yet* I felt he was really sorry. He was crying and all, so I believed him and forgave him. For the next few days, he was the model boyfriend, taking care of me and trying to make me feel better.

Hearts and flowers. That's what it was, just like the cycle-maker says. I learned about the cycle in the domestic violence group. I could see my life right now around that cycle. Things would get better for a little while, then there'd be a build-up of stress like work stuff, bills, the baby, my family, his family. It didn't take much. What I learned was that once they cross the line into the territory of physical abuse—hitting and kicking, throwing stuff and grabbing you—it just seems that every disagreement would eventually get physical no matter what I tried or didn't try to do. I always got the blame. If I didn't do whatever, he wouldn't have hit me. It was always me that got him so upset.

One time when he was mad about some baby stuff I bought without his permission, he came right up to me. He got right in my face. I knew it was coming, even though he'd promised it wouldn't so many times. I looked right at him. I didn't say a word. He grabbed me by the arm and forearmed me into the wall. He put his knee up between my legs and raised me up the wall and dropped me. I think I broke my tailbone when I hit the floor.

Marty left that night, taking the car and truck keys with him. I was stuck at home with a sore back and two crying kids. I didn't want to be there when he came back. I didn't want to, but I called Deidra to come and get me. She didn't say a thing. I'm ashamed to say that I went back. It was the baby's first birthday and Marty had rented a bounce house, inviting a bunch of his friends. He begged me to come back, so I did. The cycle began to spin around again.

Was this the last time he hurt me? *Far from it.* I left him three more times before the last. Marty tried to run me over with the truck when I left him one night with the babies in the stroller. My neighbor heard some noise and called the cops. Marty was arrested for attempted assault with a motor vehicle, DUI, reckless endangerment, domestic abuse in front of a child, public intoxication, avoiding arrest, and a couple of other things I can't remember.

Looking back now a couple of years since his arrest, I can't blame myself for not trying. I haven't told about the good times. He really could be good. That part I miss. But I don't miss the fear, his blame-game and, not to be rhymey, but the shame-game, too. I didn't want it to end like this. I didn't want Deidra and my parents to be right about him. I knew he could be good. At least I hoped he would.

The moral of my story? Trust your gut and trust your family's gut—the people you love and that you know love you. I didn't do that. I let pride and my own determination get in the way of common sense and good judgment. I loved him, I really did. I guess my hope for him to be better was more than his desire to *be better*—for me. My wise advice now? You don't deserve to be hurt or afraid in your relationship. Ever. Ever. Ever. Ever. I can't tell you about the physical and emotional scars I have. Don't wait to get out until it's too late. I almost did.

# Becky

Our beautiful little girl, Jenna, passed away at age 27. She was a loving daughter, sister, and friend. She was a wonderful wife and mother. She was everything you would hope your daughter could be. She was good and kind.

Jenna was all about falling in love. She was also a hopeless romantic. She dreamed of a marriage that had all of the elements of a fairytale: happily ever after with her *Prince Charming*. She loved everyone. She loved her family, her children, and her husband. She loved him. *She loved*. That is what she did. She loved everyone.

Jenna took her life. She left two young children and all of us. It's hard to understand how she could do this, but you will. I promise. You will.

I can only guess what many of you must be thinking as you are reading this. Believe me. We have heard it all. Comments have ranged from judgmental, condemnatory, and critical to referring to her eternal *resting place* as less than *heavenly*. People have questioned, "How could she have done such a thing?" "This was so selfish; so attention-seeking." When someone takes their life, to those on the peripheral, it is unconscionable, irrational, and completely illogical.

Suicide is most often equated and associated with mental illness, drug, and other substance abuse. Oftentimes it is seen as a conclusion to a combination of these things. People tend to speculate and surmise their own deductions, using their own personal experience or places of reference when attempting to understand something that doesn't make sense to them. Some have expressed that Jenna "must have been clinically depressed." *Depression*. That word *bristled* me every time someone used it. That word seems to cover and encompass every single sadness the world has ever known, blanketing it in a heavy, dark opaqueness in such a way that no one looks at anything else. No one even looks.

*I knew what it was, but I couldn't tell people that. I couldn't tell.* I had to listen. I listened as every time I turned around, Jenna's mental state was assessed, weighed, and determined on other people's scales of depression experience or their depression observations of someone else they'd judged and weighed in on. Some people can be very unkind. Someone said—in my clear and present presence—that anyone that does that *thing*—suicide—*is a psycho, a mental case.* Uggghhh. I was so tired of hearing what people had to say when they really and truly had no idea. They didn't know.

Then I heard what her husband had been telling people. He was saying that she had postpartum depression. *What?* In this —all of the judging and assessing—all accusing *fingers* pointed clearly far and away from him and squarely on her. With her choice to leave in this way—her own choosing—he was now that *poor daddy* left to raise two children on his own. *He was now a victim of hers.*

I knew what it was. I knew. We knew. We knew without a question. It was abuse. He had hurt her physically, emotionally, psychologically, financially—you name it. Her husband—perfect, spotless and seemingly blameless—had abused her over their seven-year marriage. It was domestic violence. That's what it was. *We knew.* Her husband had abused her. We knew, and he knew that we knew it.

There is a visual perception that we in society have about these men that hurt women. It seems people think that these men that abuse women fit a certain stereotypical physical appearance. They look like one of those creepy-hairy-smelly guys that crawl out from underneath a rock. Well, quite frankly, it is most often not this way at all.

A wide variety of visuals arise when one describes a man that abuses women. But as many of the stereotypical creepy, sleazy, and completely unsavory images come to the mental forefront, there really isn't a face that is the standard face of a domestic violence perpetrator. He could look like anyone. More often than the *low-life-scum-bag* stereotype describes, they oftentimes appear to be amazingly *perfect-on-the-outside*. Their outward appearance is most often really not too bad. They are smart and calculated. They have jobs and lengthy resumes that tout amazing feats and accomplishments. *Amazing.*

Yep. Our daughter's husband, from the outside, without that *looking-in* perspective, was the model citizen: trustworthy, loyal, helpful, friendly, courteous, kind, obedient, cheerful, thrifty, brave, clean, and reverent. That was the outward perception. He was *it*. Our daughter, according to the comments of many onlookers and her own evaluation of both his resume and his life-plan-potential, was a very lucky girl. He had it *all* going on. He did—*and he knew it.*

There is a common misconception held by many regarding domestic violence. So many hear those words, *domestic violence,* and immediately equate this concept with *physical beating and battery*. Oh, yes, this is very much so. But, the verbally mean, emotional, mental and psychological abuse in hurtful words, hateful name-calling, belittling and then the *crazy-making*—the *non-physical* abuse that comes with all of the perpetrator's head-games and manipulation—is certainly a form of violence. These words from someone that is loved and trusted are just as violent in their emotional and psychological *beatings and battery*—their detrimental impact just as devastating—as anything one might experience that is physical. *Even more so.*

We had learned much of what was happening in Jenna's very difficult marriage just prior to the time of her passing through her guarded disclosure of complicated secrets. Over the years of her marriage, we had our own questions and concerns relative to things we had observed that didn't make logical sense with our image of a *happy marriage*. She wasn't happy, though she should have been. All things considered, she should have been content, complete and happily so. But, she just wasn't.

Something was clearly wrong. As answers to our questions regarding her marriage began to unfold, we came to realize that our daughter had been abused in unimaginable ways over the course of her seven-year marriage by Jake, her *amazingly-perfect-on-the-outside* husband.

We knew what had happened, but we couldn't say anything. We had to be careful because of the sensitive nature of what we knew and the sensitive nature of the fact that she had children with him. Even in her passing, he had all control. There are no laws that hold a man accountable when his wife takes her life. He, from the outside (to those that didn't know) was—in *all* of this—a *victim* of what *she* had done. Yep. He was that *poor Daddy* left by a *crazy wife* and now with two young kids to raise on his own. We didn't know what to do. We couldn't tell. If we told what we knew—the truth—we would surely lose contact with our grandkids, children—hers—that we loved so much. If we didn't speak out in her defense, allowing his words to speak ill of her memory, no one could learn from this. Speak up and we lose what we hoped to keep: *contact with the kids*. Stay quiet and allow lies to define her and dishonor her memory: no one learns and no one makes changes. We would surely lose children so precious to us. It was a crummy dichotomy.

Well, these *concerns* or worries of ours regarding our daughter's relationship with Jake didn't immediately hit us in the face straight on upon meeting him. Yeah, he was loud and obnoxious at times, and yeah, he was overly *this* and overly *that*. Yeah, he teased with sarcasm. That bugged us. We didn't like it. But, we didn't always see it. We weren't around him all the time like our kids were. We heard about it. *They* saw it, but he was funny sometimes, and his teasing was, to them, just *his type* of teasing.

When Jenna and Jake were dating, his teasing was something that our family wasn't used to. We tried to see it as playful, perhaps, so not completely hurtful. It didn't feel good, but, to us, at the time, he was Jenna's boyfriend. Then, he became her fiancé. And it wasn't *all* bad—I mean what we knew. There were other things about him. He was driven – success-wise. He had goals and aspirations. He was from, what people had told us, a *good family*. He was talented, and, well, yes, he was a little arrogant. Really—*can you be a little arrogant?* In reality, his arrogance and his hurtful, sarcastic teasing bothered us. We were concerned. We had addressed our concerns regarding these things privately with Jenna. She explained them away as his nervousness around us. Okay, we would try to help him feel a little more at ease and comfortable when he came around. We didn't want to be critical. We wanted to be accepting, understanding, and loving. He was different than us and we wanted to be welcoming.

Alright. So you know about him, and you know a little about her—and us. Over the years, things started to become more apparent to us. He was different. It was important for us to get along with his differences. And we did our best.

Now, I'm going to jump about seven years ahead from the time that they married for the purpose of telling this story, passing through her dating and marriage, having her first baby, Lewis, and having moved several hours away from where she had grown up. This brings us to the time when I went out to help her after she had Tara, her second baby. Jenna appeared to be tired and a bit overwhelmed, yet she was so in love with this beautiful dark-haired little girl. Lewis was enamored with Tara, too.

One of the first days after I had arrived, we went to the grocery store to get a few things that I would need. While at the store, I told Jenna that I was there to help. I would be doing the cooking. I asked her to tell me what she wanted me to fix. We would get it. Well, she didn't know. She had no idea what to tell me. Really, she seemed *lost* at the store. Lost. I asked her what she would get when *she* shopped; what *she* liked to cook. She told me that Jake did all of the shopping. My first thought was, *that's odd*. He's busy working, and he does the shopping, too?

Hmmm, I thought, helpful, but a little *overly helpful,* if you were asking me. It was all so very odd to me, so I logged it.

While at the store, I had bought some Almond M&M's: one of Jenna's favorites. It was a treat I knew she would enjoy—kind of adult. Kids don't generally like things like this: nuts in their M&Ms. I liked them, too. When we arrived home from the store, I asked if we could put the candies in a bowl and put them on the counter like we would at our house, so all of us could have some. So, we did. Jake had just arrived home. He came to the counter, took a handful of M&M's and then took the bowl, placing it on the highest shelf in the cupboard. He left the kitchen without a word. I was dumbfounded. I said to Jenna, looking at the cupboard shelf high above our heads and our reach, "What in the world? I'm gonna have to get a chair ...." She didn't say anything. I noted and mentally logged that, too.

While at the store, I had purchased a big bag of chicken knowing that Jenna liked chicken. We could fix chicken *this* or chicken *that*. So, for this particular evening, I had fixed a chicken-ritz cracker casserole—something I knew that Jenna loved. It was ready to eat, just waiting for Jake to come home. The house was obviously filled with the smell of dinner when Jake walked in the door. Jenna and I were playing with the kids as we waited for Jake to unwind and get ready for dinner. I mentioned to him as he came into the house that dinner was ready when he was. It had been about 10 minutes when I smelled something cooking in the kitchen. It smelled different than what I had prepared, so I peeked in the kitchen, seeing Jake fixing a quesadilla for himself to eat. From all obvious indicators, dinner was clearly ready and waiting. I was confused. I asked Jenna what was going on. I had clearly fixed a meal that was ready to eat.

She said to me, "He likes to cook."

I said, "But I already did that."

She appeared to be a little embarrassed by what was happening. So, I asked, "Does he do this a lot?"

88

She said something that surprised me. She sighed and said, "He's a better cook than I am."

*What? Who had determined that?* So, I asked Jenna that question. *Who had determined that he was a better cook?* She looked at me and looked away. She simply said, "Jake."

My heart sank. *What kind of a husband says that?* Men don't generally care what's for dinner, as long as there is something to eat. Again, I was stunned. I logged it.

I could go on and on regarding little incidents that I had seen that were completely confusing. One of the oddest things I witnessed while I was at Jenna's house during my maternity stay involved a sandbox of sorts that she had made for Lewis for indoors. She had taken a large plastic container and she had filled it with a variety of rice and beans and then put small toys in it for Lewis to dig in. She would spread a flat bed sheet out in the middle of her living room and put the bucket there for him to play. He loved it! It was absolute genius! I wondered why I hadn't thought of this for my kids! I was amazed! When he was finished playing, we would gather up the sheet and pour the rice and beans that had escaped back into the container and put the lid on it. Easy! As we were sliding the container into the closet, I saw her turn and look at the couch. Hmmmm. There was a bean—a single bean—under the couch. Without hesitation, Jenna turned and *dove* after it. I have never seen anything like that. She dove as if to save her life! I couldn't believe what I had seen. I *logged* it.

Now, before I go on, please allow me to review these four seemingly small incidents that I had logged—and explain why they were significant and how they affected Jenna. First, being *lost* at the grocery store—this is quite typically an area of domain for many women, particularly those that shop and cook for a family. If you shop at all, you know the store you like, as you spend not only a lot of money there but a lot of time. Jenna was not allowed to shop without Jake's permission or strict adherence to his shopping *parameters.* What we later learned is that if he even allowed her to go to the store without him, he made a list, and if Jenna had deviated from *the list* and she had purchased items that were not on the list, she was in trouble. He would line up the list with the receipt as there was an *accounting* that had to be made. She had to stick with the list on product size and exactness to what Jake had determined, or she would have to *pay*. It was easier and less stressful for her to just relinquish the shopping and all of those decisions—those money-associated-tasks—to Jake. Thus, Jake controlled and made *all* of the decisions that involved family resources.

Second—the M&M's? Jake removed them from her reach as items such as this were *contraband* for her. She was not allowed to consume items with refined sugar—candy—as he was controlling her caloric consumption. This fact became apparent in a few other incidents that I also *logged* regarding his rules and constraints on her diet.

Third. When Jenna expressed to me that Jake was a better cook, two things became readily apparent to me. For one, he had diminished her self-worth regarding her ability to cook—to do something she loved—for someone she loved. Cooking, preparing meals, and feeding her family is an active expression of love for a woman. He had taken this domain and vital self-esteem building action away from her, claiming from her that ability and making it his. Whether or not a woman is a good cook or has these skills, is not the issue. If a man wants his wife to be a good cook, all he has to do is tell her that she is. If he tells her she is, he will find that she will be an amazing cook. In telling her she is good at this—like any other loving and service-oriented ability—she will do all she can to do it well, so as to make him happy. Jenna's self-esteem in this critical area of showing her love for her husband and her family had been stolen from her.

And, fourth. As for the indoor sandbox, this was something that Jenna had created for Lewis so that he could play and be a little boy in exploring and digging for treasures while she took care of the baby. He loved it, and she had lovingly created it. What I later learned and realized when I had seen Jenna *dive* after that single bean under the couch was that she was only able to do this activity under Jake's strict rules and controls. If Jake had seen that bean under the couch, the activity *was over.* Not only would the activity be curtailed, but she would suffer his discipline for her negligence. She went after the bean as if her life depended on it, because it did.

When I was in their home for that short maternity stay, I logged and noted several incidents that puzzled me. Even if Jenna had seemed a bit less than her usual *on-top-of-things-self,* when you love someone, you care about them. You don't treat them unkindly. I *logged* his responses and his words to her during basic everyday conversations. I *logged* what I saw and what I heard. My heart sank when I saw and heard it. He wasn't very nice. *Could it be him?* She was smart and accomplished and remarkably so. Why was he so unkind to her? But then, he'd do and say something nice! I was so confused! Was it her? I was back in *his* corner! I was back wondering, again, *what had happened to her.*

I returned home from this trip with so many things on my list—things I had logged—that just didn't figure with Jake's *great guy* persona. I told Bob about everything I had observed. We hadn't seen her but a few times over the three years that they had moved away. Jake had his idiosyncrasies that we had kinda realized were just him. They were *just Jake.* But, when I was there in their home, there seemed to be something else going on with him. I saw things that just weren't right, but I couldn't put my finger on it. When I shared these things with Bob, he and I were puzzled. Jake was good, even kind, one minute, then hurtful and insensitive the next. I had a hard time figuring out why he did the things and said the things to her that he did while I was there. As I tried to assess what I was seeing in his expressions to me – regarding Jenna's weakness and lacking – against his proficiency, adeptness and his strong personality, I was so confused. *He* presented as amazing and *she did not* – but I knew that she was – *or had been*. So then, what – over the years of their marriage – had happened to her? Why did he treat her as if she was so incapable and unintelligent right in front of me? He seemed to *play her* to me as deficient and incapable and I was somehow *buying* it. I was left wondering what had happened to *her*. Jenna was so sharp and so competent in everything as our daughter before her marriage. *What had happened? Was it her?*

Bob and I considered every point and each position. We tried to think of something else—anything else. But, for us, it honestly was easier to see her the way he portrayed her. Yet, my *mother instinct* told me it was something else. Again, no one, especially us wanted to believe that he was hurting her. The things she said, the way she acted—it didn't make sense. It just wasn't like her! I told Bob we needed to take our family vacation out there so he could see what I had seen. So, we did.

When we arrived at their home, Jenna literally collapsed in her dad's arms. Jake did all he could to portray her as incapable and even crazy while we were there. On our last day there, she asked if she could come home with us for the summer months. She needed help with the children. That would be good. Sure, we said. We could also get her some help and figure out what was wrong.

We wanted so much to help her get her confidence back—to get stronger. So, Bob counseled with a friend that was a doctor. We needed him to see her regarding the possibility that it might be postpartum related. I disagreed—*strongly*. My *mother-heart* and intuition told me different. I had seen things when I was in their home when I was there that concerned me, but this was not it—not this type of depression. I looked harder at the things I had *logged*. This was not depression. This was something else. Then it started to click. *This wasn't her.* As Bob and I noted her activities in our home, we realized that it really *was* something else. We didn't see what Jake had told us. She wasn't at all like he had described to us. The way she acted was completely in line with the way he was treating her.

What I had seen in her hollow countenance wasn't post-partum related depression but her reaction to her husband's ill-treatment. What I had seen in her expressions when he shouted at and belittled her was fear and confusion. Little things that she said to me, upon questioning, started to fit and filled in the blanks. There it was. I knew that it was not her. *It was him.*

Now what? When we realized what he had done to her, we had to get her help. We needed things confirmed and validated. If this was so, we needed a professional opinion and help. She needed to see a therapist and we needed to find out from a professional perspective what was going on. So, we got her in to see a therapist that was able to evaluate her using professional *tools.* The therapist concluded what we had thought, yet dreaded. He described her as having all the physical, psychological and emotional representation of a prisoner of war. He told us that, yes, she had a form of depression, but not postpartum. He said that she had *situational* depression as a result of being married to an obsessive-compulsive, controlling, abusive, narcissistic man. She was, in fact, being abused by her *perfect-on-the-outside* husband. She was a victim of domestic violence.

The therapist recommended individual counseling for her. He also recommended that there be therapy for Jake regarding his control issues and obsessiveness. Of course, we had no say in whether or not this would happen. The therapist expressed to us what was happening through utilizing the *Domestic Violence Wheel of Control.* By viewing this wheel, the therapist showed us the cycles that perpetrators go through. Seeing this, we knew that her husband would most likely *not* make the changes that he needed to make. He might stop for a little while, but Bob and I knew he would likely *cycle* again as these men do if they don't get help. He would likely continue to abuse and hurt her. We knew that Jenna was not physically or emotionally safe in Jake's presence.

As we began learning about what had happened, we felt that Jenna needed to stay with us longer than the predetermined summer months. We didn't trust Jake. She didn't either. She wanted to stay with us. When Jake came out to take her and the kids back home with him, we carefully talked to him about our concerns for her health. We felt this was safe and that we wouldn't be putting her in jeopardy by saying this. Even though we were careful in framing things as considering her mental well-being, we could tell that he was suspicions. We felt that he could see that his *private world* of secrets was quickly unraveling.

Jake went back to their home without his family. Once there, he became increasingly more hurtful and demeaning. He demanded that she get a job to pay for the diapers she was using on the children. He became more openly hurtful, threatening and difficult. We now had a battle on our hands. Her fearfulness and heartache over all that was happening were so devastating to her. She believed everything that he said in his accusations, blaming herself for all that was wrong. Jenna was heartsick and confused. Jake had robbed her of every bit of her self-esteem, destroying it. He controlled every aspect of her life from the inside to the outside. We learned that he had obsessed with the outer appearance of everything: the house, the car, the way she looked. Everything had to be outwardly, visibly perfect: skinny, well dressed (his perfect picture) with amazing children. He controlled *everything*.

We asked Jenna what she wanted us to do. We would support her in whatever she chose, but we did not feel it was safe for her or the children to return to him. She agreed. But, she knew he would be upset with her if she didn't. She didn't know what to do. She was so confused and frustrated. She didn't want divorce for her children. She really didn't want divorce for any of them. She didn't want the kids to grow up without a dad in their lives. She just needed to be a better mother and a better wife. Her self-blame was overwhelming. We told her that this—these things—were not hers. She worried about the kids. We told her that Lewis and Tara would be fine. This was not about them either.

As more and more information continued to unfold, we learned that not only had Jake been emotionally abusive and oppressive, other abuses were present in her marriage as well. We had suspected but not seen him physically harm her. So, I asked her if she had ever been physically abused in her marriage. I asked her point-blank. It was her non-answer that spoke the loudest. She turned her head, turning away, shaking her head—not to say "no," but as if to say, *"Mom, don't ask me that."* She wouldn't say anything.

I said, "Jenna. You tell me." She wouldn't look at me. I said, "Jenna. Has he ever hit you, touched you, poked you, pushed you, needled you, grabbed you—has he ever hurt you and made you feel scared or unsafe?"

She said, "Mom—" She just kept shaking her head.

I said, "You tell me."

She was crying. She said, "I deserved it."

I held her, telling her, *"You did not!"*

Yes, he had pushed, grabbed, punched his fist through the wall by her head, he had picked her up and thrown her out of a room and locked the door. This is what she dared tell us. We know that there is more than we know that happened to her.

We worked hard to strengthen her every day. Jake was coming out a month later. He had said that he missed the kids. Jenna was fretful and worried as he had been increasingly more hurtful and accusatory on the phone with her. We didn't know what to do. It felt better having him stay somewhere else and get a protective order against him, but we decided that it might be best to have him stay in our home with him under our noses. Jake would stay with us.

It was a difficult week for all of us. Jenna spoke to him regarding the possibility of divorce—a strong move for her. I was alone with him in the house one night, and he wanted to talk to me about something unkind that he had said regarding me. I hadn't heard what he had said, but Jenna had told him that I had. I guessed, as he began to explain, that she had told him that I had heard it so as to make him accountable to me for his unkindness, so I played along. I wasn't going to let that one go. He wouldn't treat me like that. Jake wanted to explain to me what he meant by his mean comment. What he expressed to me was not founded on truth, so I said to him, "Good try. *You in*? 'Cuz I've got something to say to you."

He sat with me as I told him what I had seen and what I knew from my own perspective about what had been going on, not from things she had said. I began telling him what I had observed; I didn't want to use her words and get her in trouble. I confronted him about his abuse and told him that no wife should ever be afraid of her husband. I identified scenarios that I had witnessed when I was at their home when Tara was born. As I was confronting him, Bob and Jenna, with her children, came home. Our daughter took the younger ones to the playroom, and Bob and Jenna sat across from us. Bob told me to carry on. So, I did. Jenna was in the most safe place she could be right there next to her dad. So, I let Jake have it. I identified a certain incident that I was aware of, and he vehemently denied it.

I said, "Whether you said it or not, it was implied and she believed it." I made my point, so I moved on to other things, but I logged his response for later. I told him that we loved him and that we were pulling for the marriage, but Jenna was not going home with him. He needed to re-court her and we would monitor his progress. He had some changes to make—work to do—and he needed to get some help.

So, the next morning, Jake had gone to run some errands. I asked Jenna regarding the particular incident that I had identified to Jake that night before. I asked her if it, in fact, had happened as I had said. Did it really happen as I had reported it to him? She said, "Yes."

I said, "Here you were—right next to your dad in the most safe place you could be while I was nailing your husband. Why didn't you say, 'Yeah, ya did, pal!' Why didn't you defend yourself? *Why didn't you defend me?*"

She just stood there and said, "*Mom, The price was too high.*"

I knew then that she knew very well the price for standing up for herself. She had likely *paid* that night for everything I had said.

Jake left the next day to go back home without his family. I told him again as he was leaving that we loved him, but we wanted him to cease what he was doing to her and be the husband that we hoped that he could be. He needed to get help, and we would watch him carefully. We too, wanted the marriage to work out. We didn't want unhappiness for any of them. Jake went back to their home alone—and not very happy.

When Jenna had first started her therapy, she was asked to write a letter to Jake expressing to him what he had done to hurt her. She wasn't sure that he really knew what he was doing and how he was hurting her. It was just the way he was. Her therapist said, "If he doesn't have the information, then he can't make the changes. Who is going to tell him?"

Jenna was afraid of him. Who could do it? I told her that I was not afraid of him. I had already confronted him. So, after he left, I wrote him a letter and between Jenna and I, we went over everything—every word for exactness in event and over again to see whether or not a word was too harsh or not descriptive enough, and then we read it several times. It was from me. I didn't want him to blame her. It was written in such a way that I described for him the things that I had observed, not things she had said. Later, after she passed away, we learned that she had told her younger sister, Cindy, things that she was too afraid to tell us. Cindy told us that he had told Jenna that anything she told us, he would find out. Jenna knew there would be consequences for her. She was so very frightened of him.

When the letter was completed, I said to Jenna, "So, now what? Should we send it?"

She said, "He needs to know."

When Jake received the letter, he told her that what happened in their marriage stayed in their marriage. He told her that she had been disloyal to him by telling us things. She had defiled their marriage. He told her that she didn't deserve him or the kids.

We talked to her about divorce. We told her that we would keep her with us for as long as she needed to stay—forever if she needed to. As much as we tried to help her, we couldn't stop Jake's hurtful threats and unkindness. We couldn't stop him. We also couldn't enlist help from his family, our families or anyone else. She still had a hope that he would change. We couldn't undermine her hope. If we told everyone what was happening, she would have been so embarrassed. It was hard enough on her that we knew what was happening. She didn't want divorce for herself or her children. In her heart, she wanted her marriage to work out. We had to support her wishes. We told her that we would support whatever she chose. Her hope of a marriage with a *fairytale ending* was out the window. She was living a nightmare. Her *Prince Charming* had blamed her for every problem that could be found in their marriage and their family. She saw only herself as the causal factor in her family's unhappiness.

After a very difficult phone call from Jake, Jenna explained to us the things that her husband had said to her. He had diminished her worth as a mother, telling her that he was a better mother than even she was. Over the four years since Lewis was born, he had taken her ability to mother away. She was *the stupidest mother on the planet*, Jake had said. He had convinced her that she was a lousy mother, and the kids would be better off without her. She believed him. It didn't matter what we said, he had such control over her. He had threatened, saying that if she even thought about divorce, he would easily get the kids because he could prove her incompetent and incapable and no judge would ever give kids to a stupid mother. She would lose, and she would never see them again. In her estimation, it was all her fault. She would lose her children.

When he left after the last visit, he would call and say such horrible things to her. She was crying a lot. One day when he called, I took the phone and I confronted him about what he was saying to her. He had accused her of coming home to find *a little boyfriend*—something so ridiculous and injurious to everything about her. When I spoke to him, he told me that he was her husband, and he could demand answers however he chose. I told him to stop calling. I could not see an easy reparation of the years of hurtfulness. As far as I could see, the next course of action was divorce and moving on.

"What will I do?" Jenna asked us. "Who would have me as stupid as I am?" Her self-blame permeated everything.

Then Jenna said something that absolutely floored us. She told us that *someone would have to die* for things to change from the way they were for her.

Jake's unkindness and hurtful words and actions had destroyed any hope she had for happiness and any confidence in her ability to continue as a wife and a mother. Jenna couldn't figure out how to be the two things that she desired most—a wife and mother—and be happy. She told us that he would use the kids against her and still abuse her in front of them and otherwise. They would never love her. She didn't want them growing up with images of her being beaten and called bad names. If they divorced, she knew he would paint her in a bad light. He had beaten her down emotionally and mentally so badly. She wanted so much to be a good mother, but he wouldn't let her. She told us that she couldn't imagine staying married to him, but she couldn't divorce. He would be more mean and controlling in divorce than he would be in marriage. Divorce would be so hard on the kids. They were so little. Jenna didn't want them growing up with battling parents and all of that turmoil. She said that if she disappeared, they could have a chance at growing up happy. She loved them so much. To her, she was the reason Jake got so mad. Perhaps he would be able to be nice to someone else, after all, he had threatened that he could easily replace her with someone better, smarter, more capable. Jenna wanted so much for the kids to have a chance at happiness. We tried to convince her that this wasn't the way it should go, but she felt that it would be best for her to disappear. She just needed to disappear. In her mind, logically, this was the best option for all of them. She had heard Jake tell her so very many times that everyone—himself and the kids—would all be better off without her.

We did everything we could to help her, but we couldn't stop Jake's mean threats and then, his horrible silent treatment. He had broken her heart and her spirit. A week and a half later, she hung herself. Bob found her. She was gone.

We miss her so much. It is so hard to think that for her, she saw this as the only way out, but when we look deeply at the things she went through and his visit to our home three weeks before, she just spiraled down. It breaks our hearts that as she saw it, someone had to die.

So, here we are. We have no legal rights with the kids. He's back to himself. He is a victim of Jenna's choice to leave as she did. As he tells everyone, he wasn't even there when it happened. He was actually back in their home several hours away when it happened. None of this happened *on his watch*.

Bob has expressed to people a little analogy that absolutely describes what we tried to do. He tells that we *delivered* our daughter to her husband upon their marriage as a *cup*—perfect and full to the brim. Over the next seven years of their marriage, her husband had poked holes in the cup until she came to us with very little of herself left. We tried patching the

100

holes and then filling her up each day, but each night her husband would call and poke a new hole in the cup or break open an old hole and make it so much bigger. We found ourselves patching, repairing, and filling her up so often until we felt that maybe she would be alright. When he came out in the Fall, he poked so many holes in the cup that we were losing so much of her every day. We tried repairing the holes, but they just wouldn't hold. It came to the point that all we could do was hold our hands tightly around her as best we could until the bottom fell out and there was nothing we could do.

Well, this is a sum-up of what we know. Jake and his family tell that she had severe postpartum depression. They say that her family did nothing to help her. It sure sounds better than some *battered wife thing*. All accusing fingers point to her – and us. We have no contact with the kids.

I remember a neighbor of ours telling me regarding her son-in-law who was an alcoholic and abusive to their daughter: "We love Michael, but we sure don't like what he is doing." I thought, *How can you love a guy who is beating your daughter?* Well, strangely enough, I still don't know the answer to that one. I do know that we love Jake. We know that we really are the only ones that can help him. We have to be ready to help him if and when that time ever comes. Jake needs us. He needs our help, and, more than anything, he needs our love.

We're trying our best to understand Jake. Did he know what he was doing? How could he have been so hurtful, so mean, so blatantly unkind to her? I asked her several times if her husband knew what he was doing. Did he know? Were his actions calculated, or was he foolish in his deliberate unkind treatment of her? He took every ounce of self-esteem, every ounce of worth; he robbed her of her ability to speak and even dare to think about defending herself.

So, remember how I had written, with Jenna beside me, a letter to Jake identifying the things he had done to her—the letter that we sent? We had discussed what might happen upon his receiving this. With all of the information, we determined that one of two things would happen. Either he would make the necessary changes, and then she would know where he was *at,* or he wouldn't make the changes and we would know *exactly* where he was at. One option for him would be that he would humbly beg for her forgiveness and plead with her—and us—to allow him an opportunity to make everything right. That would be noble and good. The other: he would deny all wrongdoing, turn things around, blaming her for every wrong that had happened. Each outcome had an upside and the possibility of a very difficult downside. If he chose to repent and make things right, then he would need to truly apologize for every hurtful thing, ask sincerely for forgiveness, and then she would have to be strong enough to *check* him every time he slipped back. With the other, she would know exactly where he was at in choosing to remain in his hurtful, destructive, and abusive ways. We would proceed with terminating the marriage and then move forward. We would support her with all we had as long as she needed. She agreed that this was something she could do. With Jenna's approval, I sent the letter. So, Jake had the information. He had a plan and I had even expressed our love and desire to help him. He never responded to me regarding it. We know that he chose not to speak to her. He was good at the silent treatment thing.

On that day before all of it happened—that event that determined her passing—I was in the kitchen with her discussing the options that she had in the event that Jake might seek professional help and make positive, sorrowful, and resolute changes relative to his abuse of her. It didn't seem likely that he would, but we wanted to be hopeful.

I asked Jenna, "Do you think he's mean-spirited, or do you think he's just plain *stupid*?"

She said, with a thoughtful pause, "Mom, I think he just doesn't know better."

I think she was right. He had gotten into a pattern of unkindness in humiliating her with his mean comments and the repetitive rigor of putting her down, speaking in terms using mockery and sarcasm, playing the know-it-all, and degrading her. He had developed a pattern of being mean and lost any knowledge of how to be nice. That doesn't excuse him, it's just the way it was.

With all of this said, and believe me, there is far more to this story than these pages and your heart's read of this allows, I will share this last sum-up in our daughter's own words.

I had promised you in the beginning that you would come to understand how someone could leave—take their life—as a result of the abuse and mistreatment of another. It is absolutely that phenomenon referred to as being *bullied to death*, only the bully is one who promised to love, honor, and cherish. Our Jenna is likely not the only girl that has ended her life as a result of an abusive husband or boyfriend's mean and hurtful words and actions. There are likely many, many little Jennas out there. Sadly, our daughter's feelings about herself as a result of abuse is not unique to only her. It happens more than we know or want to think about. With this in mind, let me end my writing by sharing, in Jenna's own words, how her husband's abuse affected her.

I asked her, that day before, something that I had wondered for a long time. Remember when you would play those word games where you are allowed only one word to describe something? I had wondered how Jenna would describe Jake given those parameters. So I asked.

"If you could describe Jake using one word—just one—what would it be?"

Jenna paused for a second or so and said, "Big."

Taking our assessment of Jake and his personality that was loud, all-encompassing that seemed to fill the room when he was at our home, I asked, for understanding: "Big—like, '*big-that-fills-the-room*?'"

Jenna simply stood there. She sighed, saying:
*"Bigger than me."*

# We can do this

Human nature is human nature, and different people have life experiences as a result of their families of origin, their cultural diversity and their physical and personality differences in strengths, and weaknesses: all of those things that make each one of us unique. We learn patterns that we *inheri*t or embrace in our communication styles that are either helpful or hurtful.

Difference is great and it is *terrible*. These differences that come from our life learning can influence us to act out of *selflessness or selfishness.*

As human nature goes, some life experiences in the form of *differences* offer the development of personality traits that lead individuals on a path of being self-centered and unkind, hurting and harming those around them. These individuals exhibit traits of being jealous, self-centered, insecure, needy, childish, sarcastic, greedy, narcissistic, deceitful, disrespectful, angry, inconsiderate, domineering, controlling, haughty, mean-spirited, unkind, and arrogant. They tend to leave a path of destruction as they go about their egotistical way having little or no regard for anyone but themselves and their self-absorbed neediness.

On the other hand, human nature is human nature and there are people that have developed attributes as a result of *their* life experiences that lead *them* on a selfless path of service and support. They have developed personality traits that encourage in themselves and even catalytically in others to be caring, kind, considerate, humble, gracious, patient, empathetic, charitable, sympathetic, tolerant, loyal, sensitive, warm, respectful, grateful, understanding, friendly, sincere, and genuine.

Nevertheless, these traits are not genetically predisposed in us. They are learned. We all have a choice in how we treat each other. We can choose.

So, look at yourself and see where you fit relative to the nature of your humanness. We can all do a little better. We all need kindness and support from time to time as life challenges go.

If, perhaps you see yourself, or someone you love, in the collective run of personality traits that include the words, *self-centered* and *unkind*, quite possibly several of those other traits are familiar, as well—maybe not to you—but they are likely familiar to people close to you. If you can recognize yourself and recognize these, it is not too late to make some serious character adjustments. Your words and your actions are in jeopardy of harming, hurting, even causing the destruction of those you care about. If you desire to make changes, you will need some help and support. It is a difficult thing to do, but it is possible. Seek help in individual therapy. Here again, the Domestic Violence Hotline can serve to guide you to a reputable professional therapist that works specifically with this concern in your area. Seek help through your clergy. They can also direct you in finding help in making personal changes, oftentimes through opportunities of service to others. Change, redemption, and repentance are for everyone and certainly possible when one is penitent, contrite, and sincerely sorrowful. It is never too late to make an honorable attempt at righting a wrong. A *mighty change of heart* is the only reliable cure and solution for this. This comes through personal recognition, sincere remorse, a desire to do better, and actively implementing these changes.

It is very difficult to be successful in making these critical life changes all by yourself. Success comes from being accountable. It helps when there is someone in your life—a *helper*—that can support you in your changes and, quite frankly, hold you accountable.

If, perhaps you see yourself in the run of *descriptives* that include the words, kind, considerate, and caring, keep on doing and keep on being. The world needs so many more like you. Charitable goodness and gratitude most often beget these traits in others. Your influence can help others in dire need of your support in the face of trials and discouragement.

No one should ever feel diminished and insignificant because of another's dominance and imperious control. Anyone that treats another in such a way so as to make them feel small so that they can feel big is, in fact, weak, puny, and insecure. There is nothing big, strong, or honorable about this.

You, the women I have collected these stories for, are better—far better than living your lives under the cruel and ruthless authoritative control of an insecure, self-centered man. I hope to offer *hope* that in seeing your life through a lens of truth and the offering of hands and even shoulders of support, change can make a difference in your life. For yourself, your parents, your friends, and your children—everyone that sincerely loves you—you can't afford to live like this or even *die like this*. Domestic violence is wrong. If this is happening to you, get help and get out. If you are doing this, get out and get help.

No one should make another person feel small so that they can feel big.

The bottom line of the *last word*:
*You* are *Bigger than he.*

# Cycle of Abuse

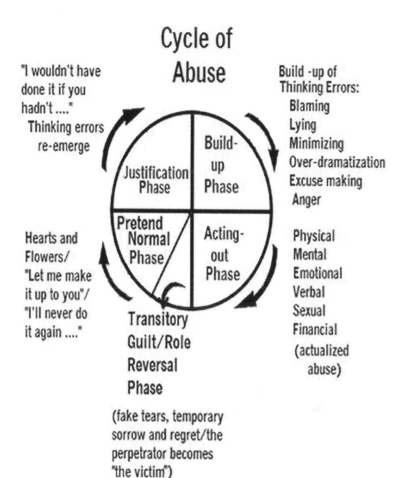

"I wouldn't have done it if you hadn't ...."
Thinking errors re-emerge

Build-up of Thinking Errors:
Blaming
Lying
Minimizing
Over-dramatization
Excuse making
Anger

Justification Phase

Build-up Phase

Pretend Normal Phase

Acting-out Phase

Hearts and Flowers/
"Let me make it up to you"/
"I'll never do it again ...."

Physical
Mental
Emotional
Verbal
Sexual
Financial
(actualized abuse)

Transitory Guilt/Role Reversal Phase

(fake tears, temporary sorrow and regret/the perpetrator becomes "the victim")

# Tell Your Story

If you have a story that needs to be shared, told, and heard, here is a safe place to begin writing it. Write what you feel safe telling and keep writing. When you feel safe enough to share it with someone, find a good listener. Find someone that you feel safe telling. You are not alone. Telling is a powerful thing.